# When Heaven Feels Distant

# When Heaven Feels Distant

TYLER J. GRIFFIN

SALT LAKE CITY, UTAH

Visit us at DeseretBook.com

---

**Library of Congress Cataloging-in-Publication Data**

Names: Griffin, Tyler J. (Tyler Jay), 1973– author.
Title: When heaven feels distant / Tyler J. Griffin.
Description: Salt Lake City, Utah : Deseret Book, [2018] | Includes bibliographical references and index.
Identifiers: LCCN 2017040981 | ISBN 9781629723976 (paperbound)
Subjects: LCSH: Mormons—Conduct of life. | Suffering—Religious aspects—The Church of Jesus Christ of Latter-day Saints. | Christian life—Mormon authors.
Classification: LCC BX8656 .G76 2018 | DDC 248.4/89332—dc23
LC record available at https://lccn.loc.gov/2017040981

---

Printed in the United States of America
PubLitho, Draper, UT

10 9 8 7 6 5 4 3 2 1

*Dedicated to all who struggle and to the Lord of mercy, who is mighty to deliver*

# Contents

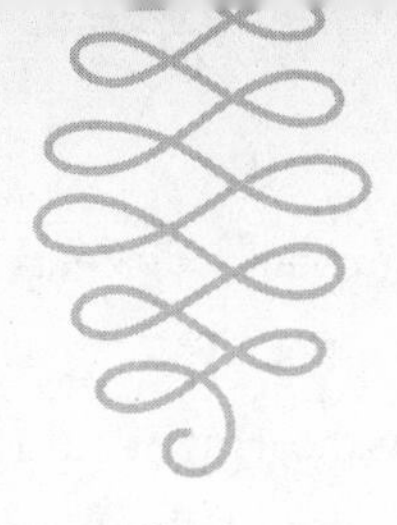

# Acknowledgments

I have many people to thank for helping me throughout this journey. Bob Millett and my current dean, Brent Top, gave me the encouragement I needed to begin the process. Lisa Roper worked with me to identify the topic and has given me helpful, formative feedback all along the way. Tracy Keck helped me polish the final drafts of the manuscript.

My dear wife, Kiplin, helped and encouraged me from start to finish. On occasion, she would stay up late at night, reading the manuscript to give suggestions. Much of what is included in this book represents shared experiences with her or insights received *from* her. Heaven rarely feels distant as long as she is by my side.

My father-in-law, Emery Crook, has been through this manuscript multiple times. He has the gift of patience and an eye for clear, concise, and complete writing. He was gracious enough to give me multiple rounds of feedback. He was also instrumental on many occasions in helping me align individual sections of the book with its overall purpose.

When Brad Wilcox joined our faculty in BYU's Department of Ancient Scripture last year, I was grateful to be assigned as his faculty mentor. I knew a lot of mentoring would take place, but based on his life experience I had no doubt about who would benefit the most from our interactions. When he heard I was writing this book, he asked if I would like him to review it. I assumed he would read a few chapters and give me some experienced-author recommendations. Was I ever wrong! Brad printed all 150+ manuscript pages and spent hours marking up every one with insightful suggestions for improvement. His feedback was astute and influential. Thanks for the mentoring, yet again, Brad.

My brother-in-law, Adon Crook, also helped me with formative feedback. It didn't take him long to realize that I am more comfortable as a teacher than as an author. He helped me translate my classroom ideas into appropriate book structures. I'm grateful for his shaping and undiluted feedback and helpful recommendations.

I am grateful for editorial and grammatical feedback from my sister, Dana Rasmussen. Two of my nieces, Alexia Morris and Aleni Rasmussen, were also kind enough to read through the manuscript and share their thoughts with me. Davis Agle tracked down all of the book and scripture references to verify accuracy.

I'm also grateful for the many people mentioned in the book who were willing to share their stories and insights with me. I am especially grateful to Tim Turner and Floyd and Carole Burnett for being willing to help me tell their story in the introduction. I know that process was not easy for them.

Most of all, I acknowledge the goodness of God. Nothing I have written or accomplished is of any value without Him. His feedback and corrections along this journey, while being the most painful and hard to take, have been the most helpful and shaping of all.

INTRODUCTION

# I Don't Understand, But I Will Trust

As a young child, did you ever wander off and get lost? How did you feel? As you grew older, did you ever experience complete rejection after striving with great effort to achieve something? Do you remember how that felt? Have you ever found yourself facing a seemingly impossible task? Has your faith ever been seriously challenged by a difficult question? Have you had a relationship fail? Have you been diagnosed with a serious disease or had a major operation? Have you lost a loved one? What thoughts and emotions do you experience at times like these?

Chances are, your attention turns heavenward, either looking for answers and strength or because you feel the need to vent frustration or anger.

We have all felt the raw emotions of grief and despair that typically accompany traumatic experiences. In these stressful circumstances, we may begin to feel as if the heavens have withdrawn, leaving us to face our difficulties alone. But something deep inside our hearts whispers otherwise. It's inspiring to meet people who have found ways to tune into *that* whispering voice in the face of trials. Such stories touch us in a way that causes heaven to feel closer and helps us discover greater meaning and motivation in our own struggles. Those experiences are sacred ground. I have met many people who have shared their stories and left me better than they found me. Tim and Karen Turner are an especially powerful example of this.

The Turners' family wasn't typical. They had six children ranging in age from seven to fifteen. Five of the children were challenged, with a diverse range of abilities. Jessica, their oldest, felt out of place because she was the only child without a serious disability. Emily was wheelchair bound and nonverbal with cri-du-chat syndrome. Dallin was autistic. Katelyn, Joshua, and Megan, the younger three, were adopted siblings who all faced serious challenges including reactive attachment disorder, oppositional defiance disorder, and lingering complications as a preemie born four months early. Needless to say, Karen had her hands full with homemaking and taking care of the daily needs of their children while Tim was at work.

Despite the effort associated with vacationing, the Turners enjoyed traveling and decided to take a coast-to-coast Church history trip. In June of 2010, they left their home in Oregon, dropped Emily off in Salt Lake City with Tim's sister, stopped at Martin's Cove to pull handcarts, and visited the pioneer museum at Winter Quarters.

While driving through Iowa, they ran into a torrential downpour. Suddenly the van hydroplaned, spun out of control, and slammed into a concrete wall. Tim, Jessica,[1] and Joshua sustained life-threatening injuries, while the other three children escaped with little harm. While in the ER, Tim learned he was being treated for multiple wounds, including a neck broken in five places, a severe concussion, and a broken arm. His physical injuries, however, were completely overshadowed by his anguish when the news arrived that Karen, his wife of eighteen years, had not survived the crash.

Within a day, extended family members gathered in Iowa to help in the initial wake of the accident. On the second day, most returned to Utah, taking the three uninjured children with them. Karen's father, Floyd, and Tim's younger sister, Tressie, stayed behind to help.

Quickly, the crushing weight of guilt settled in for Tim. In the midst of his shock, internal agony, and intense physical pain, he was flooded with numerous questions and faced critical decisions—all while recovering nearly two thousand miles away from home. While lying in the ICU, he ached to comfort his young family, spread across several hospitals—and states—over the loss of their loving mother. The immensity of funeral arrangements, surgeries, and rehabilitation, combined with feeling responsible for destroying his family, took its toll. For six days, Tim's strength continued to decline because he was not able keep any food down. Tressie insisted that Tim try to eat, but nothing would stay down. Finally, she asked him if *anything* sounded appetizing.

"The only thing that comes to mind is banana bread," Tim responded.

"But you don't even like banana bread," was Tressie's reply.

"I know, but it's the only thing that sounds good right now," he said.

Tressie then informed Tim that she had a fresh loaf of banana bread back in Joshua's room at the children's hospital. One of the sisters from the local ward had just delivered it. She told Tressie that she had received an impression that morning to bake banana bread. She had no idea why the prompting had come but had acted on it anyway.

Tressie rushed over to the children's hospital and returned quickly to present Tim with the gift. As he opened the still-warm package, the aroma of fresh-baked banana bread filled the hospital room *and* his heart. For the first time since the accident, his stomach didn't turn at the smell of food. He broke off a little corner of the bread, tentatively put it to his mouth, and slowly chewed, savoring every moment. In that instant, Tim felt that he had tasted much more than a freshly made and miraculously delivered loaf of banana bread; he had tasted the reassurance and love of his Father in Heaven that he so desperately needed. The loaf of banana bread was not just the workmanship of a charitable woman's hands; this was the workmanship of *God's* almighty hand in the life of one of His children who was hurting deeply and was in desperate need of a miracle.

*He had tasted much more than a freshly made and miraculously delivered loaf of banana bread; he had tasted the reassurance and love of his Father in Heaven that he so desperately needed.*

Tim was able to nibble small chunks of that bread for the next six days while his strength, confidence, and will to move forward with faith slowly returned. This woman's bread did not miraculously solve Tim's problems, nor did it remove the many obstacles strewn along his road of recovery. But each bite of that heaven-delivered loaf was a symbolic manifestation of the "bread of life" for Tim.

Tim never met the dear sister who was God's instrument in this miracle. He doesn't even know her name. To this day, she likely has no idea what her selfless act and the simple loaf of bread accomplished.

At the time of these events, my family and I lived in the same ward as Tim's mother- and father-in-law, Carole and Floyd Burnett. They were deeply grieved at the loss of their daughter. They ached for Tim and the children and invited them to stay with them to help with healing and recovery before returning to their home in Oregon.

Tim told me his story after church that first Sunday after he arrived. There he sat, in a neck brace and cast, with six children who all needed a high level of care and support, and yet, he radiated a quiet confidence and profound faith. I marveled at this. He didn't know how things were going to work out, but he knew the Lord would never forsake him, and that gave him the determination to move forward, trusting in the Lord.

## About This Book

How are people like Tim able to maintain such incredible faith when heaven seems to be so distant? How do they turn *trials* into *triumphs* and *tests* into *testimonies?*[2] This is not done through earthly means. In fact, I don't believe that people change because of things they see or hear alone; they ultimately change because of things they *feel.* This is not possible without the help of a merciful God. It is the Lord who gives us the assurance we need to keep going when tragedy and heartache become, by all earthly measures, insurmountable. Only the Lord could touch Tim's heart in a way that would help him face the future with such a high level of hope in the face of such debilitating adversity. Victories like Tim's teach our hearts things that words cannot adequately tell—and yet, we try to tell them anyway. Such is the overarching intent of this book.

*I don't believe that people change because of things they see or hear alone; they ultimately change because of things they* feel.

One of the first lessons I learned as a young husband was that my wife didn't need me to solve her problems. Early in our marriage, she helped me understand the difference between offering sympathy and giving solutions. As our relationship has matured, we have grown to discover a third possibility we now add to the list. During hard times, we ask each other, "Do you need sympathy, solutions, or support?"

With this book, I seek to offer readers a measure of all three. There are times when we need sympathy. It is often reassuring to know you are not alone when you feel deeply hurt or completely forsaken. I have included real-life and scriptural examples of inspiring people, like Tim, who found themselves dealing with trials and struggles of every variety. You are not alone. Your difficulties and pains are real. There are many who have gone before whose experiences can help us feel less isolated as we each take our turns passing through our own furnaces of affliction.

There are also times when we need solutions and correct principles to help us act appropriately to solve our problems. In these pages, I seek to reaffirm and fortify the most important solution of all, faith in Christ *amid* the storms of life. Whether our feelings of isolation are caused by death, disease, broken promises, doubt, fear, unrealized dreams, or any combination of life's tribulations, the resolution is always the same: "There shall be no other name given nor any other way nor means whereby salvation can come unto the children of men, only in and through the name of Christ, the Lord Omnipotent" (Mosiah 3:17). There are many places in the book where the reader will find principles that can be put into practice. Most of the teachings and doctrines I will share are taken from the scriptures and real-life experiences and presented in a way that I hope can be applied in a wide variety of situations.

Perhaps most of all, this book seeks to support you in your efforts to submit to the Lord and trust Him, *especially* when heaven feels distant. Even though most of our struggles are not as profoundly difficult as Tim's, we all experience heart-wrenching challenges that cause us to ask the difficult questions: Why is life so hard? What is all this suffering and uncertainty for? The Lord has helped me in the past; where is His steady, guiding hand now? Why do I feel so forsaken and alone? Where are heaven's promised light, direction, and tender mercies—especially when I am trying so hard to do what's right?

## "I Don't Understand"

Perceptions of a distant heaven are usually complex and don't always come with easy answers. In fact, sometimes they don't come with any answers at all. As feelings of isolation from God linger, frustration and anxiety can increase. Some choose to stop keeping certain commandments and gradually abandon prayers, fasting, and scripture study. Others may continue to go through the motions of Church membership but feel largely unfulfilled by those activities and end up feeling robotic or spiritually numb. Some abandon their faith altogether or fight against it. Still others believe heaven is withdrawn because they will never measure up.

And yet, some people find a way to draw nearer to God, even as the world would claim that heaven is retreating from them. Such was the case with Tim Turner and his in-laws, Carole and Floyd Burnett. Karen's passing was not the first untimely death in the Burnett family.

A few years earlier, in 2007, Floyd and Carole's son, Matthew, had been an active and bright medical student living in Rochester, New York. Everything changed for him and his family when he was diagnosed with cancer. After a valiant battle, the cancer began to prevail. Matt was granted his medical degree in August of 2008, and within a month, he was placed on hospice care. His wife, Christine, felt that they would rather be close to family for his final months of life, so they moved with their four small children to Utah to live with his parents. Matthew kept fighting from September to January, when he was lovingly and submissively laid to rest by his grieving wife, children, and parents.

It was only seventeen months later when Carole and Floyd received the news of the terrible accident in Iowa that claimed the life of Matt's older sister, Karen. As the news of her death spread through our ward that Sunday, we all felt the shock and anguish of this tragedy. When my wife, Kiplin, found Carole in the hallway, she could not find any words to say to comfort this dear mother. She just put her arms around Carole and they cried together. Carole, in a moment of profound honesty, simply said, "I don't understand." Kiplin felt the raw agony behind those simple words, and yet what she felt even more was Carole's intense trust in the Lord and submission to His will. In that moment, Kiplin felt as if Carole had given *her* strength and comfort.

"I don't understand": simple yet genuine words. Words spoken not out of anger or resentment. Words not flippant or defiant. But words of submission and trust. They reflected a complete surrender to the Lord. Neither Carole nor anyone else really understood why these things were happening, but the trial did not harden her heart—it remained soft. She and her husband recognized that long before Matthew and Karen had been delivered to their arms, they had belonged to Heavenly Parents who loved them perfectly. God could have prevented either untimely death, but He didn't. The Burnetts didn't know all of the answers, but they knew the Lord!

At Matt's funeral, Floyd reminded the congregation of the truth found in Job 1:21: "The Lord gave, and the Lord hath taken away; blessed be the name of the Lord." This degree of faith was also appreciated by Elder Neal A. Maxwell when he shared the story of nine-year-old Melissa Howes, whose father was dying of cancer. Just before her father's passing, Melissa offered the family prayer and pled, "Heavenly Father, bless my daddy, and if you need him more than us, you can have him. We want him, but Thy will be done. And please help us not to be mad at you."[3]

In this book, my hope is that you will open channels of communication for the Holy Ghost to teach both your mind *and* your heart how to look for the Lord's hand even when it seems withdrawn. We will examine scriptural principles that, when applied, can help us learn and grow when we are called out of our comfort zones and sent into the unknown or when our timetables don't correspond with Heaven Standard Time. We will look at parallels between Heavenly Parents and earthly parenting. We will look at the marvelous gift of ambiguity and how it empowers our agency. We will explore lessons we can learn from the struggle between our flesh and our spirits. We will look at principles to guide our interactions with loved ones who struggle. The last two chapters contain final principles and thoughts for helping us draw nearer to heaven and build our faith in God.

Throughout life's journey, I stand with Carole in acknowledging, "I don't understand." But I also stand with her and Floyd and with Tim, Jessica, and the other children in choosing to trust in the will and timing of Heavenly Parents who love us more deeply than we can now comprehend.

In the words of one of my favorite people, who also experienced more than his fair share of extreme difficulties: "My God hath been my support; he hath led me through mine afflictions in the wilderness; and he hath preserved me upon the waters of the great deep. He hath filled me with his love. . . . O Lord, I have trusted in thee, and I will trust in thee forever" (2 Nephi 4:20–21, 34).

Despite all that we do not understand, the Lord has given us many answers and revealed true principles to guide us on the strait and narrow way that leads to eternal life and a fullness of joy in this life and the next. It is my hope that you will know *and* feel how much you are loved and how close the Lord really is as you read these words—*especially* when heaven feels distant!

CHAPTER 1

# Heaven Is Closer Than It Seems

*"O God, where art thou? And where is the pavilion that covereth thy hiding place?"*
*—D&C 121:1*

"How do you feel about your relationship with Heavenly Father?" I asked my twelve-year-old daughter Kinley one afternoon. She looked sincerely at me and then began to tell me about a dilemma she had been wrestling with for a few months. She shared that she had prayed many times with all her heart for guidance on what to do, but no answers came. She fasted; no response. She pondered the issue during her scripture study, at church, and while attending the temple to do baptisms for the dead; nothing. She felt no heavenly guidance on this matter for weeks, despite her diligent and faithful efforts. As she was telling me this story I began to worry about how her faith would be affected if this heavenly silence continued much longer.

In my moment of quiet concern for her, Kinley began to weep. Choosing her words carefully, she said, "Dad, these experiences have actually made me trust Heavenly Father *more.* I have come to know Him better and love Him more through this struggle." She then related how just a few days prior, the Lord had finally given her an answer. It was different from what she had anticipated, and it was given in a way she had not expected. But after what seemed like an eternity, her answer *did* come! It was clear, direct, and unmistakable for her. My daughter treasured her new understanding, in large part because of the process she went through to receive it.

Kinley's story may seem inconsequential compared to the mountain of trials that so many others face, but her struggle and subsequent breakthrough at that stage of her life were significant and tailor-made for *her.* That experience became a treasured part of a solid foundation for her developing faith.

It was one thing for her parents and teachers to share lessons *about* God, but it was an entirely different matter for her to be taught directly *by* Him. Through family discussions and church classes, her mind had grasped many truths about the infinite nature and capacity of the Governor of the Universe. But through Heavenly Father's personalized tutelage and Kinley's diligent faith, He touched her heart with His perfect love in a direct and personal way.

*"No matter what happens in your life, always remember that Heavenly Father holds worlds without number in His hands, but He holds you in His heart!"*

A few months after that experience, Kinley wrote a priceless note of encouragement to her younger brother, who was struggling with feelings of self-doubt and discouragement. She concluded her note with something I had shared with her many months before but thought she had forgotten: "No matter what happens in your life, always remember that Heavenly Father holds worlds without number in His hands, but He holds *you* in His heart!" These were not hollow words for her. They represented an authentic glimpse into the heart of a young girl who loved her Heavenly Father and had been shaped by Him through her feelings of distance from Him for many weeks.

This experience taught Kinley a lesson that numerous people throughout time have also discovered; heaven is closer than it feels.

Whether we find ourselves on a dark and stormy sea, wrestling with complex questions, striving to see the Lord's hand, desperately seeking a miracle, or trying to better understand God's attributes and purposes, He is never far away!

## Two Storms

One night nearly two thousand years ago, Jesus boarded a small fishing boat to cross the Sea of Galilee. The craft was manned by experienced men who were intimately acquainted with that sea and such vessels. Despite their experience, the tempest that awaited them carried a fury that caught them off guard. The winds were so violent and overpowering that "the waves beat into the ship, so that it was . . . full" (Mark 4:37). In the disorienting darkness of the night and the unrelenting pitching of the nearly overwhelmed boat, the terrified disciples turned to Jesus for deliverance. Strangely, He was not distressed in the least. In fact, their Master was sleeping in the back of the boat.

*Jesus calmed much more than an extremely rough sea that night; He calmed a raging storm* within *His fearful disciples.*

For the disciples, it is clear that two storms raged that night: one on the sea and another in their hearts. The *external* forces intensified as *internal* despair. Their terrified cry, "Carest thou not that we perish?" contrasted with Christ's authoritative command: "Peace, be still" (Mark 4:38–39). Jesus calmed much more than an extremely rough sea that night; He calmed a raging storm *within* His fearful disciples.

Additional storms would arise again on the Sea of Galilee, indicating that the physical effects of Christ's miracle would not last forever. The spiritual effects of His miracle, however, could stay with His disciples the rest of their lives and into eternity. Perhaps the most wonderful thing about this miracle is that it is not bound by time. The command, "Peace, be still," echoes through the years until it can calm even the storms we face today. Jesus' presence does not guarantee a smooth ride through our sea of life, but heaven is never distant as long as we are in the same boat with the almighty Son of God.

## Our Storms

We were not in that fishing boat two thousand years ago, but our journey through life shares many parallels with that perilous night. Jesus invites us into a covenant relationship. We symbolically get into the boat with Him and launch out into the deep. Many of our problems arise when we embrace false assumptions and have unreasonable expectations of what such a journey will require. Many of us assume that diligent discipleship will guarantee a life of ease and minimal difficulties. The reality is that progression in the gospel, by design, is messy and muddy, riddled with storms of varying intensities. Elder M. Russell Ballard taught, "We are on the old ship Zion. . . . [God] is at the helm and will stay there."[1] The test is to stay in the boat with the Lord, rather than assume we can do better by abandoning ship and trying to swim to safety on our own.

*Although our storms are different from those on the Sea of Galilee, our solution is identical.*

Human tendency causes us to panic and become overwhelmed when difficulties mount. Often, our knee-jerk response is to question God's motives, concern, and love for us as we ask, "Why does the Master sleep?" Just as He was near His disciples throughout the tempest, He is never far from us, *especially* when our personal storms rage. Jesus' presence protected them from drowning, but it did not protect them from getting soaked and stretched to their limits. Although our storms are different from those on the Sea of Galilee, our solution is identical–turn to the Lord in faith and hold on; waiting, trusting, even knowing that He *will* help us according to His own purposes and timing. He never forsakes us. President Howard W. Hunter put it this way: "If our lives and our faith are centered upon Jesus Christ and his restored gospel, nothing can ever go permanently wrong. On the other hand, if our lives are not centered on the Savior and his teachings, no other success can ever be permanently right."[2]

## "Acquainted with Grief"

Jesus was not a stranger to sorrow and grief. He experienced them throughout His life—not just in infinite proportions during His atoning suffering. When He learned that John the Baptist had been killed by Herod Antipas, He surely felt the customary grief that accompanies the tragic death of a loved one. However, this loss would likely have been even more painful to Jesus considering John's unique role as the Savior's forerunner. The Baptist's mission was to prepare the way for Christ's coming. With John's martyrdom, those preparations were now being made in the spirit world, reminding Jesus that His own life would soon end as well. It is not surprising that "When Jesus heard of it, he departed thence by ship into a desert place apart" (Matthew 14:13). Even *He* felt the desire to escape the crowds and to deeply connect with Heavenly Father.

His attempt to find privacy, however, was unsuccessful. "When the people had heard [of his departure], they followed him on foot out of the cities" (v. 13). As the ship came into the shore, Jesus "saw a great multitude" (v. 14). Most of us would have guided the boat to the other side of the sea to find solace. But Jesus "was moved with compassion toward them, and he healed their sick" (v. 14). He spent that day binding up broken hearts and healing suffering that was far less intense than His own. There is no mention of anyone asking Jesus how *He* was feeling that day. People brought *their* needs and desires to

Him, and He met their needs without drawing any attention to His own. After healing the crowd, He miraculously fed them with five loaves and two fishes.

We might ask, "Why didn't God give Jesus a break—a time for his heart to heal?" Is it possible that Heavenly Father sent the multitudes to Jesus that day as part of a healing and consoling process? Although later that evening, Jesus was finally able to go up into the mountain to pray alone (see v. 23), perhaps He was never more connected with heaven than when He was surrounded by hungry crowds, ministering to their needs.

Might this same principle also apply to parents, bishops, auxiliary presidents, and all who work tirelessly to give selfless service to others? They experience pains, anxieties, and pressures in life. They yearn for "alone time" to connect with heaven. Instead, they are barraged with requests and concerns that need their immediate attention. Like Jesus, rarely are mothers or fathers asked, "How can I help you? What do you need?" And yet, despite limited opportunities to have quiet connection with the Lord, they *still* find ways to address the myriad demands life requires of them. Could it be that considering our limited time, energy, and abilities, these feeding-the-5,000 moments are in fact heaven's way of connecting with us?

*Could it be that considering our limited time, energy, and abilities, these feeding-the-5,000 moments are in fact heaven's way of connecting with us?*

From John the Baptist's death forward, the injustices and difficulties Jesus faced increased. He progressively did more good but received mounting rejection in return. However, He did not allow the world's growing disapproval of Him to decrease His connection with Heavenly Father.

Moments before Jesus' final condemnation, Pilate presented a choice to the leaders of the Jews. Which person did they want released and forgiven of all charges: Jesus or an infamous prisoner named Barabbas? Serving as a stark contrast to the Savior, Barabbas had been charged with sedition, murder, and robbery (see Luke 23:18–19 and John 18:40). The people were asked to choose between an insurrectionist and a peacemaker, one who took life and one who gave it, one who stole that which was not his own and one who freely gave what He had to others. The crowd demanded that Barabbas be released and Jesus be crucified.

*Those feelings of isolation and longing could be the very catalyst that will, in time, lead to our sweetest and most poignant connections with heaven.*

For many years, I was filled with unkind feelings toward Barabbas. He was guilty and was released, while Jesus was innocent and was punished. Then one day I realized that, symbolically speaking, this was *my* story! *I* am Barabbas. I am guilty and deserve punishment yet get released because Jesus suffered in my place.

I've heard it said that a perfect man at an imperfect trial was found guilty so that one day an imperfect man at a perfect trial could be found not guilty. In truth, few things connect us more intimately with heaven than our struggles and our abject need for the Savior's grace, mercy, love, and help. Those feelings of isolation and longing could be the very catalyst that will, in time, lead to our sweetest and most poignant connections with heaven.

## Extending Our Limits

Not all afflictions involve bad things happening. Feelings of isolation from heaven can also arise when we desire blessings, answers, or directions that don't seem to come. As my young adult students face their "decade of decision,"[3] I frequently hear from some who feel lost and alone. I received the following email from one young woman. It is shared with her permission:

"The past few months I have felt distanced from God. I still feel the Spirit here and there, but I don't feel close to Heavenly Father as is typical for me. It has been hard to face these decisions while I am facing this feeling of being somewhat apart from my Heavenly Father. I know I am imperfect, but I have not done anything that would make me unworthy. I keep my covenants faithfully, I attend my church meetings, I go to the temple often, and I study my scriptures and pray every day. Yet, this feeling of distance has been my constant companion. This past Sunday evening as my week was coming to a close, this feeling of separation from the Lord became completely agonizing to me. Although I knew it was not so, I felt abandoned by Him. I felt left alone. And I wondered why, at such a crucial time in my life, it seemed as if He had just gone on vacation. It brought me to tears as I began to wonder when I would ever feel close to Him again. I was not questioning my testimony; I just wanted this situation to be fixed. Monday night I received a blessing and was assured that the Lord has never left my side."

This pattern of being stretched, tried, and tested beyond what we think reasonable is a common theme in the scriptures and in the lives of people who love the Lord and are loved by Him.

## Look for His Hand

There is no simple formula to have problems suddenly dissolve or to make feelings of isolation disappear. We can benefit, however, from taking a few steps back and considering the big picture. One way to do this is to read the scriptures, learn about other people, and look for patterns of the Lord's guiding hand in *their* lives, thus making it easier to find that same divine mercy and grace in our own struggles.

One of the most oft-read verses of the Book of Mormon is 1 Nephi 1:1. As a teacher, I have noticed most of my students zone out when reading: "I, Nephi, having been born of goodly parents, therefore I was taught somewhat in all the learning of my father; and having seen many afflictions in the course of my days, nevertheless, having been highly favored of the Lord in all my days; yea, having had a great knowledge of the goodness and the mysteries of God, therefore I make a record of my proceedings in my days."

My students usually focus on the first few words and then either skip or skim the rest, overlooking some important principles. Perhaps you, like them, have had the experience of reaching the end of a page of scripture only to realize that you have no idea what you just read. When we have no specific purpose or focus while reading scriptures, our minds naturally wander. Read 1 Nephi 1:1 again. Notice that Nephi had great blessings, but he also had seen great afflictions. Sound familiar? Is that perhaps how Nephi came to the knowledge of God's goodness that he was now going to record for us?

This same principle of really *looking* and not zoning out applies to our lives in general. If we skip or skim, we are less likely to notice the Lord's guiding hand in all the miraculous details of life. President Henry B. Eyring shared one way that he is able to focus his attention by looking for heaven's influence every day. He asks the question, "Have I seen the hand of God reaching out to touch us or our children or our family today?"[4] When we actively look for the Lord's hand in our lives, we are much more likely to find it than if we passively wait for Him to get our attention.

*When we actively look for the Lord's hand in our lives, we are much more likely to find it than if we passively wait for Him to get our attention.*

## "Daddy, Are You Looking at Me?"

Even when we seek and find His merciful hand, we are not guaranteed that our problems or concerns will instantly resolve. We do, however, gain a certain level of comfort knowing that the Lord *is* watching us and is fully aware of our situation. Elder Quentin L. Cook shared an experience of a time when he and his two small sons got stuck in a June blizzard at Donner Pass. When they were finally towed to safety, he called his wife, who asked to speak with her two boys. His youngest son summed up the perilous journey by telling his mother, "Hope ya know, we had a hard time!"[5]

Elder Cook remarked, "I could tell, as our three-year-old talked to his mother and told her of the hard time, he gained comfort and then reassurance. Our prayers are that way when we go to our Father in Heaven. We know He cares for us in our time of need."

Many years earlier, Elder Marion D. Hanks spoke of a grieving young father and his two children on the evening after his wife's funeral.[6] The father gently carried his little girl to her bed after she fell asleep. His little boy asked if he might be able to sleep in his father's room that night. As they silently lay there in the dark, the lad spoke: "Daddy, are you looking at me?"

"Yes, son, I am looking at you," was the father's reply.

The young boy then sighed and fell asleep. The father waited a moment and then, with heartfelt cries, called out, "God, are you looking at me? If you are, maybe I can make it. Without you, I know I can't."

Elder Hanks testified: "Our Heavenly Father *is* looking at us . . . and sometimes he weeps for us."

## God of Miracles

That level of love and concern is occasionally manifest through the Lord's miracles. In Matthew 8:2–4, we read that Jesus was surrounded by a multitude of people when a man with leprosy approached. In

Jewish culture, it would have been inappropriate for this man to be in the vicinity of non-lepers due to his "unclean" condition. Most of the people around Jesus would have likely shrunk back in revulsion at the leper's approach. There is, however, no sign of Jesus backing away from this man who came with a heartfelt plea.

The leper petitioned, "Lord, if thou wilt, thou canst make me clean." The initial phrase, "if thou wilt," implies that this man was completely submissive and willing to accept whatever Jesus decided. These words imply that the man would have still worshiped the Lord even if Jesus had not granted a cleansing miracle that day. The leper's genuine meekness is a great example to follow when we seek to connect with the Lord and His miracles.

Typically, the scriptures don't tell us *how* a phrase is spoken; they give us only a translation of *what* was said. The leper's second phrase provides an instance in which the "how" of speech can add depth to our understanding and appreciation of the story. The leper said, "Thou canst make me clean." By placing the emphasis on different words in that phrase, the leper becomes more relatable to us and his struggles become more relevant. Each variation of emphasis carries unique lessons for us. My favorite set of words to accentuate are *thou* and *me*. Most disciples firmly believe that Jesus Christ has the power to heal others or perform miracles for them. The difficulty is *personalizing* His mercy and grace: "*Thou* art the only one who has the power and the love to make *me* clean and whole." In that moment, the infinite Atoner becomes our intimate Savior.

Total submission of will, followed by absolute faith in Jesus' healing ability, allowed for a life-changing miracle for that leper two thousand years ago: "And Jesus put forth his hand, and touched him, saying, I will; be thou clean. And immediately his leprosy was cleansed" (v. 3). People in the crowd that day must have cringed to see Jesus reach out and touch the leper, but there was no hesitation from Him.

Leprosy of old has many symbolic ties to our sin and spiritual impurities today. We are not so different from this leper. We are all hopelessly unclean and unable to heal ourselves. There are times in life when we feel unworthy to ask for Jesus' cleansing help. At other times, we might feel inclined to back away from those who approach us for help in overcoming their struggles with sin. If this leper can teach us anything, it is that even the best Saints are still "unclean" and need the purifying touch of the Savior's merciful hand.

*If this leper can teach us anything, it is that even the best Saints are still "unclean" and need the purifying touch of the Savior's merciful hand.*

## How We Perceive God

In the parable of the talents (see Matthew 25:14–30), Jesus revealed great insights into God's character and our relationship with Him. In this story, the master gave different amounts of money to three servants. In giving out the five, two, and one talents, he was not concerned with sameness because each received "according to his [own] ability" (v. 15). He did not overwhelm any of them by giving them more than they could handle. Talents represented a certain weight of money, but in this parable, they can be symbolically seen as anything received from the Lord, including our testimonies, families, possessions, money, or abilities. The first two servants doubled their talents by investing them. When the master returned, they each gave their increased talents to him. His response was the same to both of them: "Well done, thou good and faithful servant . . . I will make thee ruler over many things" (v. 21, 23). The lord did not keep the talents they returned to him; he gave them back to these two faithful servants. If we were to ask either of them to describe their master, we would probably hear words such as *compassionate, kind, loving, generous, big-hearted,* or *merciful.*

The parable took a drastic turn, however, when the third servant entered for his moment of accountability. His words were filled with apprehension and fear as he approached the master: "Lord, I knew thee that thou art an hard man, reaping where thou hast not sown. . . . And I was afraid, and went and hid thy talent in the earth" (v. 24–25). This servant couldn't wait to return the lord's talent because of the burden it represented. Notice the contrast between this man's judgment of the lord's character and the perception of the first two servants. Each experienced exactly what he anticipated. The first two servants judged the lord righteously, they worked hard for him, and their perception of him was reciprocated in a grace-filled reward. The third servant judged the lord to be harsh and cruel, a person to be feared, and that is exactly what he encountered (see v. 26–30).

Our perception of God has a direct effect on the way we live, which determines what kind of an experience we will have when we are ultimately judged. If our perception of God is like that of the first two servants, our lives will be governed by faith. If, however, we view God the way the third man did, we will make decisions driven by fear. This causes us to see the Lord as a ruthless and angry being who is looking for any reason to punish us for our mistakes and shortcomings. We will picture Him frowning down on us. We will visualize Him holding in one hand a book with our name on it and in the other a permanent marker, waiting for the chance to make yet another condemning mark against us.

*Our perception of God has a direct effect on the way we live, which determines what kind of an experience we will have when we are ultimately judged.*

The way God will judge us in the future is largely determined by how we judge Him in the present. Heaven will draw increasingly closer as we discover His true character and attributes and emulate Him. We will progressively sense His encouraging smiles and outstretched arms of invitation; we will live by faith and rejoice in the miraculous gifts He so graciously gives us.

The Lord's love is easy to feel when everything is flowing smoothly in our lives. His commandments are easier to follow when we are basking in heavenly light. Discipleship gets more difficult, however, when clouds of opposition, rejection, temptation, or loss eclipse that warm light. Fortunately, there are principles we can apply when we find ourselves in dark or difficult places or when mounting resistance meets diminishing strength. Despite these struggles, like Kinley, we can all remember the almighty God of the universe holds worlds without number in His hands—and as your Father, He holds *you* in His heart!

CHAPTER 2

# Into the Wilderness to Find God

*"The people that walked in darkness have seen a great light."*
*—Isaiah 9:2*

Ups and downs are part of nearly every aspect of life. C. S. Lewis' famously devilish character in *The Screwtape Letters* taught his understudy nephew, a devil named Wormwood, that human "periods of emotional and bodily richness and liveliness will alternate with periods of numbness and poverty."[1] At one point in the book, Wormwood's "patient," a man living in England during World War II, seemed to have lost all hope. Seeing this man's despair, and with no apparent help coming from God, Wormwood began thinking the battle for the man's soul was nearly won. It was in this context that Screwtape explained a phenomenon regarding the highs and lows of human life. He called it the law of undulation.

No mortal escapes the realities of this undulation, with its cheery heights interspersed with equally dreadful depths. Screwtape's next insight is for all who feel they have spent more than their fair share of time in the valleys of life. He explained that God "relies on the troughs even more than on the peaks; some of his special favourites have gone through longer and deeper troughs than anyone else."[2] Screwtape explained that devilish causes are in greatest peril when a person who is full of despair in a deep gorge cries out for help from

God, receives no identifiable response, and *still* chooses to obey. These experiences are tremendous spiritual victories and bring a person increased capacity to resist the devil's power.

Staying faithful during these low times, however, is not easy. The deepest valleys of life are dark and difficult places. Care should be taken when making major life decisions in those valleys when we are emotionally upset, physically hurting or exhausted, or under major pressure. In those situations, our vision is often limited and our ability to think clearly might be clouded. Reactionary decisions made when we are in life's troughs are not visionary and usually lead to regret. If we obey in faith and wait for the darkness to pass, however, a ray of hope always returns. Once we find ourselves standing in the light again, as faint as it may be, we are in a much better position to make wise and inspired decisions regarding our life, faith, and long-term relationships.

*Reactionary decisions made when we are in life's troughs are not visionary and usually lead to regret.*

Throughout our life, the Lord gives us many opportunities to practice principles of faith and obedience. The Lord will call us many times to leave our comfort zones and enter wildernesses where we will be stretched beyond our current capacity, be faced with shaping opposition, be asked to endure intense ups and downs, and grow as we seek God and find Him in some unexpected places.

## Comfort Zones and Growth Zones

Consider how often inspiring stories begin with the main character on a symbolic mountain peak. He has all that he needs. Life is flowing along smoothly. He is content in his comfort zone. However, the peace and predictability don't last long before he is faced with a new, unpleasant challenge. To succeed at this undertaking, the character must step out of his comfort zone and find his way in an unknown wilderness—a growth zone. It is in the wilderness that he realizes he can't survive on his own. The soul stretching that takes place involves a heart-wrenching process of leaving the pleasant predictability of his comfort zone and finding a way to conquer the unknown. There is often little growth in the comfort zone and little comfort in the growth zone.

Ultimately, this is typical of our own story. Before coming to earth, we lived in our heavenly home. Imagine how wonderful it must have been to live with our Heavenly Parents, receive divine instruction from Them, and be nurtured under Their perfect care. But we could only learn so much and develop so far in our spirit-body condition. We had to leave home and enter mortality to continue progressing. It is in the wilderness of earth life, in a body of flesh with all of its imperfections, that we can learn about God and ourselves in ways that were not possible in heaven before we were born.

In the beginning, Adam and Eve walked and talked with God in the Garden of Eden. They were limited in what they could learn about themselves and about Him in that state. They made a conscious choice to partake of the fruit, and it resulted in expulsion from their comfort zone. In contrast to the garden, this earth is a dreary wilderness with weeds, thorns, pains, and death. Instead of looking at their fallen state as a curse, however, Adam and Eve saw it as a blessing, a growth zone, allowing them to progress. Eve described their new opportunities by saying, "Were it not for our transgression we never should have had seed, and never should have known good and evil, and the joy of our redemption, and the eternal life which God giveth unto all the obedient" (Moses 5:11).

*It is in the wilderness of earth life, in a body of flesh with all of its imperfections, that we can learn about God and ourselves in ways that were not possible in heaven before we were born.*

## Become Something

The Book of Mormon begins with the Lord commanding Lehi to leave his house, lands, gold, silver, and precious things and flee to the wilderness. Lehi's son Nephi informed us of his father's diminished situation by simply stating, "And my father dwelt in a tent" (1 Nephi 2:15). This verse is short in words but long in symbolic meaning. The land, gold, silver, and precious things Lehi left behind in Jerusalem could never compare with the blessings God had waiting for him in the New World. Lehi's tent became the difficult bridge between what was sacrificed and what was promised. In many ways, Lehi's tent represents *our* mortal existence here on earth. That tent is a symbolic stepping-stone between what we left behind in heaven and what we seek to obtain in *our* promised land, the celestial kingdom.

> *Did the Lord send Lehi's family into the wilderness to help them* get somewhere, *or to help them* become something?

Did the Lord send Lehi's family into the wilderness to help them *get somewhere,* or to help them *become something?* The answer is both! If transporting Lehi's group to the New World had been God's only purpose, He could have greatly simplified the process detailed in 1 Nephi. Consider how easy it would have been for God to instantaneously transport all the people and the brass plates across the ocean to the promised land. This would have bypassed the wilderness wanderings, backtracks, ship-building, and perilous ocean voyage.

God could have given Lehi's group less adversity along the way. They could have awoken to find a caravan of camels waiting in their front yard, all loaded with food and provisions for the long journey. The Lord could have prevented the need for two return trips to Jerusalem; an angel could have guaranteed that Zoram and the plates would be waiting for them along the roadside; God could have easily transported Ishmael's family to Lehi's tent site as well. The Lord could have provided food for the group throughout the trip and prevented broken bows, raw meat, or Ishmael's death. They could have arrived at the seashore to find a miraculously constructed ship, loaded and ready to transport them across the water.

Obviously, arriving in to the promised land was only part of what the Lord intended for this group. The same is true for us. Getting to heaven is important, but location alone does not bring eternal happiness. We already lived in heaven with perfect Parents, but that was not ultimate happiness for us because we were not fully like them. For a chance to gain a physical body, cultivate divine attributes, gain crucial knowledge, and establish eternal relationships, we were willing to leave their presence and experience mortal life.

God *could* make everything flow smoothly for us, but He doesn't. He could instantly answer every question we ask and grant every request we make, but He doesn't. He could prevent all heartache and loss from occurring in our lives, but He doesn't. He could ensure that none of our loved ones stray from His fold, but He doesn't. He could end all doubts and arguments in an instant, but He doesn't. He could stop all abuse and prevent people from using their agency to hurt others, but He doesn't. He could miraculously transport all of us to heaven in an instant to live with Him again, but He doesn't.

Like all great historical heroes, we must face the specific wilderness God has prepared for each of us, press forward toward our own promised land, and strive to develop godly attributes throughout the journey. These soul-stretching and character-shaping growth zones are one of God's gifts to us, His children.

## Nevertheless Moments

Revisiting Nephi's opening verse, we find two phrases connected in a cause/effect relationship by the word *therefore*: "I, Nephi, having been born of goodly parents, *therefore* I was taught somewhat in all the learning of my father." Like the Lord, Lehi did not try to teach his children everything he knew about every subject. He taught them a little bit about everything he knew. This technique encourages discovery and activates agency in wilderness settings. There is a big difference between learning from our own experience versus passively being taught something by someone else. Elder David A. Bednar said, "The most important learnings in life are *caught*—not *taught*."[3]

In the second part of verse 1, Nephi informed us that his life had not always been easy: "Having seen many afflictions in the course of my days." Rather than dwelling on the difficulties of his life, however, Nephi shifted the focus by saying: "Nevertheless, having been highly favored of the Lord in all my days." Whatever follows the word *nevertheless* gets greater emphasis in a sentence. In this case, the Lord's goodness was never less than Nephi's afflictions. How much would Nephi have known about the goodness of God if his life had always been comfortable and predictable? Like Nephi, we can find peace through seeing our trials as opportunities to practice the "nevertheless principle" and focus on the Lord's goodness rather than choosing bitterness and resentment because things aren't working out smoothly for us.

*Like Nephi, we can find peace through seeing our trials as opportunities to practice the "nevertheless principle" and focus on the Lord's goodness rather than choosing bitterness and resentment because things aren't working out smoothly for us.*

## "Don't Close Any Doors!"

A few years ago, I was teaching at the LDS Institute of Religion in Logan, Utah. I enjoyed my students, colleagues, and projects. From my perspective, things could not have been better. Then one day, two professors from BYU showed up to observe my class. Afterward, one of them asked if I would consider the possibility of teaching at BYU. I smiled and opened my mouth to say I was not interested, when I felt four words enter my mind with force: *Don't close any doors!*

One thing led to another until I was invited to join the Ancient Scripture faculty at BYU. My wife and I fasted and prayed about it. At the advice of a close friend, Mark Weiss, we invited our children to join us in that fast so they could receive their own witness of what the Lord wanted for our family. The answer was unanimous; we needed to let go of the familiar and move into the unknown at BYU.

Early in the spring of that year, we began to prepare to sell our house. We talked to the realtor about our desire to sell in the late spring or early summer to allow plenty of time to settle into a new home well before the start of fall semester in late August. As summer approached, we had already lowered the asking price a few times but had received no offers. We kept lowering the price and making improvements to make our home more marketable. We kept fasting, praying, and hoping to find a buyer, but none came. After July passed, we started to feel panicked and forsaken. Our prayers increased in frequency and intensity. We had no idea what to do with school starting in less than a month. I worried that I didn't have enough faith to receive the miracle we so desperately sought. I began feeling that I was letting my family down, but my wife kept focusing me on the things we could control.

With only two weeks remaining before the start of school, our prayers for deliverance were answered, but in a vastly different way than we had expected. Rather than getting a miracle offer to buy our house, I was offered a basement room in a house close to BYU. Brother Moon, my high priest group leader, knew of our situation. He informed me that his parents would be happy to have me stay with them in their home in Orem during the weekdays so I could be close to my new job at BYU. The Moons became the Lord's miracle for me and my family that semester until our Providence house sold in mid-December.

It was not pleasant being away from my wife and children. That experience stretched me and it stretched my wife and family. We learned things about ourselves in that wilderness that we never would have discovered if the Lord had left us in our happily predictable comfort zone. While this trial was not nearly as severe as what many others face, it was nonetheless a difficult challenge for us.

That experience humbled us and required us to learn how to graciously receive service and charity from others. The love and kindness we experienced from so many good people did not take away our trial, but they made it bearable and even sweet on many occasions.

We will never forget one particular Sunday, late in November. We returned home from church to find a fully adorned Christmas tree along with other decorations in our front room. A few Relief Society angels knew that all of our Christmas decorations were hopelessly buried in the back of a large storage shed awaiting our move. Walking in the front door that day, my family saw much more than a tree, a nativity set, and garland; we saw the merciful hand of a loving Father in Heaven reminding us that we were not forsaken.

At the outset of this struggle, all we could see was a closed door—an unsold house. As things played out, however, God opened many doors for us, each one a reflection of His perfect love. The Moons, the Relief Society sisters, and so many others became those open doors of heaven for us. They provided ways for us to accomplish what was necessary while allowing the Lord to shape and polish us in the process. We are forever grateful to Heavenly Father for giving us what we needed rather than what we wanted.

Similar lessons are symbolically taught in Lehi's dream in 1 Nephi 8.

Lehi's vision began in a "dark and dreary wilderness," where he saw a man "dressed in a white robe" (v. 4–5). This unidentified man came and stood before Lehi and bade him to follow. But as he followed, he remained in the dreary waste "for the space of many hours in darkness." Why wouldn't this man have led Lehi more quickly and directly to the path, the rod, and the tree of life? Lehi's long journey through that particular wasteland may have been a required part of Heavenly Father's plan for him that could not be short-changed. If that is the case, it was a merciful Lord who ensured that Lehi would not walk alone during those dark hours in such a dreary and difficult place.

*We are forever grateful to Heavenly Father for giving us what we needed rather than what we wanted.*

How we respond in life's troughs is a better indicator of our development as disciples of Christ than how we react on life's peaks. Like Lehi in his dream, when we press forward, *especially* when the road ahead is dark and uncertain, we learn to trust in the Lord to guide us, we recognize His hand through the selfless service of others, and we become an extension of heaven when He helps us lift those around us on the path.

## A Sacrifice of Bread

I will never forget a lesson I learned on my mission in Brazil from a humble man named João who felt he was sinking into a difficult trough. My companion and I arrived at his house for an appointment with his brother, who was not a member of the Church. João looked worried as he told us that his brother had been called into work and would be unable to join us that day. The two of them worked at the same place, and João informed us that he feared they would both be losing their jobs soon due to cutbacks. We felt bad for them but didn't know how to help. We shared a brief message and prayer and as we got up to leave, João's wife handed me a bag containing a fresh loaf of bread. Their children were obviously hungry, and they eyed the bag with longing. I tried to graciously turn down the offer by asking João and his wife to feed the bread to their children, but João insisted that we take the bread.

I had what I thought was a flash of inspiration when I suggested that we all sit down and eat the bread together. Then João stepped forward and with pleading in his voice said something like, "Elder Griffin, you don't understand. My family and I need the blessings of the Lord now more than ever before. Will you *please* take the bread?" My heart changed in an instant. I told him we would be happy to take the bread if he would allow us to offer one more prayer. He agreed. We knelt down and poured out our hearts to God in behalf of that dear family. Our prayers were answered, and João did not lose his job.

I ate a lot of bread on my mission, but none tasted better to me than that loaf did on that day. It had been infused with a humble family's faith and consecration in the face of a poignant trial.

## Ever-Present Opposition

Elder Dallin H. Oaks taught, "From the beginning, agency and opposition were central to the Father's plan and to Satan's rebellion against it."[4] These two opposite forces can be seen throughout the scriptures.

Immediately before the First Vision, Joseph experienced the wrath of the devil. He recounted: "I was seized upon by some power which entirely overcame me, and had such an astonishing influence over me. . . . Thick darkness gathered around me, and it seemed to me for a time as if I were doomed to sudden destruction" (JS–History 1:15). Why would the Lord allow the devil to exert such dreadful influence over this young man who was simply seeking to know which church to join? One answer could be that he needed to experience the power of both extremes—ultimate evil along with ultimate good. When people insisted that Joseph's vision was of the devil, the Prophet could say he was acquainted with Satan's power too, and the vision was definitely *not* from him!

Moses also faced the power of the devil immediately after speaking with God face to face (see Moses 1:1–12). He instantly recognized the difference between God's glory and Satan's counterfeit. He asked the devil, "Who art thou? For behold, I am a son of God, in the similitude of his Only Begotten; and where is thy glory, that I should worship thee?" (v. 13). This stark contrast was instructive for Moses. He continued, "Where is thy glory, for it is darkness unto me? And I can judge between thee and God" (v. 15).

For three days and three nights, Alma the Younger was "racked, even with the pains of a damned soul" (Alma 36:16). Immediately after this intense suffering, he was forgiven and granted a fresh start on life. He described the transition from trough to mountain peak as follows: "There could be nothing so exquisite and so bitter as were my pains. Yea, and . . . there can be nothing so exquisite and sweet as was my joy" (Alma 36:21).

## Variations in Life's Valleys

Occasionally, some people experience low points that seem to last a lifetime. Sister Becky Reeve is an extraordinary Saint who was in a car accident while serving her mission in New Mexico in November 1962. That accident left her paralyzed from the neck down. Medical professionals gave her little hope for anything beyond a few painful years with no physical capacity. In her totally paralyzed state, Becky decided that the only thing left in her control was her thoughts, and those were understandably bleak. But Becky chose to turn her heart and mind to the Lord, to trust Him and serve Him the best she could. This decision brought her a sustaining witness that the Lord was fully aware of her and her situation. She knew that He would deliver her from her wilderness according to His will and timing (see Mosiah 7:33).

Becky convinced herself that instead of fulfilling her dream to be the very best missionary and then the very best mom in the world, she would now become, in her own words, "the very best cripple in the world."[5] She focused on what she *could* do in her condition rather than lamenting what she *couldn't* do. She has far outlived and outperformed every negative prediction and dire prognosis, and she is the first to acknowledge that the Lord has never forsaken her. For over fifty years, He has not seen fit to take away her dark and dreary wilderness, but He, like the white-robed man in Lehi's dream, has been by her side through every step of that difficult journey. Becky has proved that it is possible to suffer intensely for prolonged periods and still thank the Lord for His merciful blessings.

*It is possible to suffer intensely for prolonged periods and still thank the Lord for His merciful blessings.*

At times, troughs that have the potential to be severe pass on their own without much help from us. A few years ago, our daughter Eleesia began experiencing headaches, extreme dizziness, ringing in her ears, major stomach cramps, impaired motor skills, and nausea. Over the course of a few weeks, the symptoms became more severe, and we began to fear the worst. Multiple trips to various medical specialists produced no diagnosis. Some doctors feared cancer or an autoimmune disease. Eleesia endured many procedures and invasive exams that stretched over many months. Our prayers and pleadings became deeper and more heartfelt as we braced for the dire results each test might reveal. As each result came back negative and her symptoms worsened, the intensity of our prayers and efforts to find and resolve the problem increased.

Of times like this, Elder David A. Bednar has asked a critically important yet counterintuitive question: "Do you have the faith not to be healed? If it is the will of our Heavenly Father that you are transferred by death in your youth to the spirit world . . . do you have the faith to submit to His will and not be healed?"[6] We had no idea how Eleesia's ordeal would end, but we had to wrestle with all possibilities. After much soul searching and seeking to lay our will on the altar of the Lord, we finally got to the point that we were ready to accept, on faith alone, whatever the outcome may be. We would face the possible outcomes of Eleesia's condition with absolute trust in the Lord.

Imagine our joy when Eleesia's painful symptoms began to wane for no apparent reason. Her condition slowly began to improve, and eventually all of the symptoms were gone. To this day, we still don't know what happened or why she had to pass through that particular trial.

There is no clear answer for why the Lord chose to take away Eleesia's suffering while letting Becky Reeve bear her paralysis for over five decades. Healing is not a result of desire, faith, and prayers alone, or Becky would have been walking soon after her accident. Something much grander is at play in these situations. Regardless of the physical outcomes, our difficulties can serve to soften our hearts and make it easier for the Lord to mold us in the way that fits His eternal purposes for us. The key is to not focus so much on what happens *to* us but rather what happens *in* us.

*The key is to not focus so much on what happens* to *us but rather what happens* in *us.*

## Placement of the Rod

Some of life's troughs are caused by personal choices that lead to sin. What begins as a "go-with-the-flow" moment of indiscretion can quickly turn into a flood, sweeping us or a loved one downstream, out of control. In those situations, it is helpful to remember an often overlooked detail from Lehi's dream, wherein he saw the path, the rod of iron, and the tree of life. The location of the rod is peculiar. One would expect the Lord to place the path and rod well away from the depths of hell, symbolically represented by the river of filthy water.[7] But rather than separating the good from the evil, Lehi tells us that the rod "extended along the bank of the river" (1 Nephi 8:19). This implies that the river of filthy water was right next to the path that led to the tree, with only the rod of iron separating the two.

If we take the view that we are always on the path, pressing forward in righteousness, then this placement of the iron rod makes no sense. If we are honest with ourselves, however, we will be able to think of times when we have strayed off the path and into that river of sin. I like to think that it was a merciful God who placed the rod on the river's bank so that anybody seeking forgiveness and deliverance would be able to reach out and grasp it before being swept further downstream toward destruction.

Jesus asserted, "I am the way, the truth, and the life" (John 14:6). This declaration matches the symbols in Lehi's dream. Jesus is figuratively the path (the way), the rod (the truth), and the tree (the life). From this perspective, we can now visualize Jesus, represented by the iron rod, standing between the path and the filthy river. He is there to help those who are progressing toward the tree of life. But He is also there ready and able to pull all who reach out to Him from the merciless river.

One group of travelers in Lehi's dream reacted strangely once they arrived at the tree. This group "came forth and fell down and partook of the fruit of the tree" (1 Nephi 8:30). This portrays a highly unusual sequence of events. As the people came forward, they fell down. The *last* thing they did was partake of the fruit. Traditionally, people who want to eat fruit from a tree reach up and then partake. One possible explanation for this strange order of actions could be that the tree in Lehi's dream isn't a literal tree. If it is a symbol for the Savior, then it makes sense why people would come into His presence, fall down, and there at His feet, partake of His fruit—perfect love through His infinite Atonement. As we press forward through all the troughs and peaks of life, we will eventually arrive at that great day when we too will fall at His feet and partake of His sweet fruit.

*As we press forward through all the troughs and peaks of life, we will eventually arrive at that great day when we too will fall at His feet and partake of His sweet fruit.*

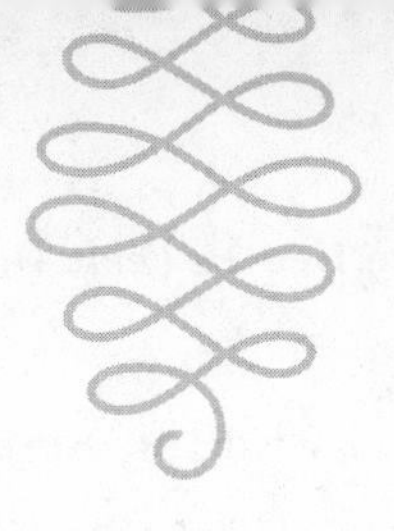

CHAPTER 3

# Cosmic Clocks vs. Earthly Wristwatches

*"In all the important decisions in our lives, what is most important is to do the right thing . . . at the right time."*[1]
*—Dallin H. Oaks*

When Peter and John went to the temple as recorded in Acts 3, they saw a familiar sight: a man born lame who had been carried to the Beautiful Gate every day to beg for subsistence. He asked alms of Peter that afternoon. Rather than supplying food or money for a day, Peter commanded him to rise up and walk. More than forty years of lameness was overcome in one miraculous instant. The man didn't tentatively stand up and stagger around; leaping up, he walked into the temple with them, praising God.

This lame man's miracle is unique in a few ways. He had begged daily at the temple for many years. It is likely that Peter and John would have passed by him on numerous occasions. It is also reasonable to assume that Jesus had seen this man on many visits to the temple during His life and ministry. It is possible that this man had seen or at least heard of Jesus' healing capacity, and yet he had not been the recipient of one of the Savior's miracles. Perhaps it was a matter of trusting God's timing. This man could have justifiably felt sorry for himself and seriously wondered whether heaven was aware of his situation. Through this miracle, Peter gained much-needed strength and experience as the Lord's instrument. The public nature of this miracle, combined with the Apostles' testimony of Jesus' Resurrection, led 5,000 people to believe (see Acts 4:1–4).

*God is not bound by time like we are. His hand can be clearly seen on the face of His cosmic clocks as He perfectly orchestrates matters of timing in our life.*

Elder Neal A. Maxwell taught, "Strange, isn't it—we who wear wristwatches seek to counsel Him who oversees cosmic clocks and calendars."[2] God is not bound by time like we are. His hand can be clearly seen on the face of His cosmic clocks as He perfectly orchestrates matters of timing in our life. Because of that perfect perspective, the Lord often delays responses, shapes circumstances, provides means for us to sacrifice, and answers prayers precisely when those things will be the most beneficial for our eternal well-being.

## Delayed Responses

Few things are more frustrating than finding ourselves in a critical situation and feeling unable to get a quick solution out of the Lord. For instance, Nephi faced a perilous situation in 3 Nephi 1, when the people he loved and served were threatened with being killed. Tension had built over many weeks and months because of the yet unfulfilled prophecies of Samuel the Lamanite. The wicked had finally appointed a day when all believers would be put to death if the sign of Jesus' birth did not appear (see 3 Nephi 1:4–10). With time running out, Nephi showed great concern for the safety of his people, although his own life was also surely threatened. "He went out and bowed himself down upon the earth, and cried mightily to his God in behalf of his people, yea, those who were about to be destroyed because of their faith in the tradition of their fathers" (v. 11).

We may think it would have been better for the Lord to clearly reassure Nephi months before this point. Instead, His answer was delayed. Even after Nephi began his prayer, God postponed His response until the end of the day: "And it came to pass that he cried mightily unto the Lord all that day; and behold, the voice of the Lord came unto him" (v. 12), promising that the sign would be given that very night (see v. 13). Thus, Jesus began His life with a miracle that symbolically foreshadowed His greatest miracle of all—saving people from death.

What difference did this delayed response make for Nephi? Did he appreciate the answer more after having to plead and worry so much before receiving it? Was he more likely to remember the lessons God was teaching him and his people due to the process he'd had to work through? Only the Lord knows why this faithful prophet had to plead for months leading up to that point, followed by painstaking hours of imploring all through that day before the answer was granted.

Enos is another good person who prayed mightily before receiving an answer. Enos had likely been praying for a remission of his sins in the weeks and months before the day he described in his book. After praying all day and into the night, he reported, "There came a voice unto me, saying: Enos, thy sins are forgiven thee, and thou shalt be blessed" (Enos 1:5). At first pass, it seems to latter-day readers that Enos was privileged with a supernatural experience of hearing the audible voice of the Lord. A closer study reveals the possibility that Enos, unlike Lehi, Nephi, and Jacob before him, received something more similar to what many of us experience today. In verse 10, he says, "While I was thus struggling in the spirit, behold, the *voice of the Lord came into my mind again*" (emphasis added). How easy would it have been after praying all day and night to just conclude that the voice in his mind was simply his own thoughts rather than the words of the Lord? Perhaps it was the diligent effort over time that made this answer not only more valued but also more recognizable.

## Shaping and Saving

Another example of the Lord's timing at work is when Peter and the other Apostles were laboring against contrary winds on the Sea of Galilee (see Matthew 14). They had been rowing for many hours in the night before Jesus finally came walking to them on the water just before dawn. He could have come to them much earlier to rescue them from their intense toil. He could have also calmed the storm and changed the fierce, opposing wind to a gentle breeze blowing in the right direction. He did neither. Once again, the Lord demonstrated that He is more interested in shaping us than He is in providing us a pain-free life of instant solutions to our problems.

Notice Isaiah's emphasis on timing when he wrote: "For a *small moment* have I forsaken thee, but with great mercies will I gather thee. In a *little* wrath I hid my face from thee *for a moment*, but with *everlasting* kindness will I have mercy on thee, saith the Lord thy Redeemer" (3 Nephi 22:7–8; emphasis added). These verses are applicable not only to the house of Israel; they also apply directly to each of us in our individual struggles.

*The shaping tests we face will not last forever, but the Lord's kindness will.*

Jesus quoted Isaiah further: "For the mountains shall depart and the hills be removed, but my kindness shall not depart from thee, neither shall the covenant of my peace be removed, saith the Lord that hath mercy on thee. O thou afflicted, tossed with tempest, and not comforted!" (3 Nephi 22:10–11). The shaping tests we face will not last forever, but the Lord's kindness will.

## Timing of Obedience

After the Lord brought the children of Israel through the Red Sea on dry ground, they journeyed through the wilderness to the southern border of the promised land. Moses sent twelve spies into the land to better know how to take over the region (see Numbers 13–14). After about forty days, the spies returned bearing clusters of fruits and reporting that it was a land flowing with milk and honey. They also reported finding giants on the land, making themselves feel as small as grasshoppers in comparison. Ten of the spies judged the opposition to be too great to conquer. This caused many to murmur against Moses yet again for bringing them out of Egypt with a promise of a new land that now seemed out of reach. Had they learned nothing in their miraculous escape from Egypt?

Of the spies, only Joshua and Caleb stepped forward and boldly declared: "If the Lord delight in us, then he will bring us into this land, and give it us; . . . Only rebel not ye against the Lord, neither fear ye the people of the land; . . . the Lord is with us: fear them not" (Numbers 14:8–9). These two valiant men tried to persuade the people to follow their prophet, believe in the promises of the Lord, and faithfully move forward. The people responded by looking for stones to kill Joshua and Caleb. Their lack of faith provoked the Lord, who refused to allow them entrance into the land of promise. They would have to return to the wilderness and wander for nearly forty years, during which time all the adults except Joshua and Caleb would die, leaving the Lord's promises to be fulfilled in the next generation.

The morning after Joshua and Caleb's declaration, a large group of Israelites arose and prepared to go forth to battle. Moses questioned them, and they acknowledged that they had sinned in not following his counsel the day before so they were going to make it right by fighting that day. He warned them not to go to battle, but they went anyway. The Canaanites defeated them and chased them out of the land. Ironically, they blamed the Lord and Moses for their failure. What a difference a day can make in following the Lord's direction! Had they gone to battle the day before, the story would likely have had a different ending.

Jacob, in the Book of Mormon, referred to this story when he taught his own people about partaking "of the goodness of God, that they might enter into his rest" (Jacob 1:7). For Jacob, that promised land of rest was heaven. What would the ten spies say if we asked them to tell us about trying to enter heaven? After all, it *is* a land that flows with eternal milk and honey, but the opposition in getting there is great. There are giant trials and temptations to overcome, and the difficulties are numerous along the way. Consequently, many people choose to give up, allowing the enormity of the opposition to overpower their faith in the Lord and negate the assurance that the Lord is well able to deliver us as promised. God's prophets never guarantee a path of ease, but they always instill confidence in the Lord's promises–hence the need to stay current with the Lord's will for us *today*, not last week, last year, or last century.

*God's prophets never guarantee a path of ease, but they always instill confidence in the Lord's promises—hence the need to stay current with the Lord's will for us* today, *not last week, last year, or last century.*

Our own expectations are a potential problem, even when we do follow the prophets or act on impressions of the Spirit. Even if the Israelites had followed Moses' counsel in the first place and fought the Canaanites, it is unlikely that the battle would have been without some pain and loss. Taking over the land would have likely been a struggle. As disciples, we should make offerings to the Lord without demanding how or when He should respond. Elder Neal A. Maxwell wisely counseled us, "Don't wait too long to find the altar or to begin to place the gift of your wills upon it! No need to wait for a receipt; the Lord has His own special ways of acknowledging."[3]

## Sacrifice without Expectations

While I was on my mission, a bishop told me the story of a recent convert who was an older widow living in the river bottoms. In Brazil, these locations would flood at least once a year, destroying almost everything. Because of this, people were allowed to build at will, without having to pay for the land. Shacks were usually thrown together from scrap pieces of wood and tin.

The bishop went to visit this widow shortly after her baptism and was distressed to see her meager living conditions. She lived in a tiny shack with an old mattress on the ground for a bed, a few pieces of clothing, a large bowl for a sink, and a propane tank with a screw-on top for a stove. A large stump served as her only chair. Her table consisted of two sawhorses with three slats of wood across the top. The bishop resolved to begin helping this widow by replacing her meager furniture, one item at a time.

That Sunday, the bishop announced to the ward that there was someone in need of a small kitchen table and asked his ward members to contact him if they had one to spare. After the meeting, this widow approached him and said that she had heard the announcement. She said it broke her heart to think of someone not having a table for their meals. She then asked the bishop to come by her house and pick up her makeshift table and give it to the person in need. She self-consciously apologized for its condition but reasoned it would be better than nothing. She told him how good the Lord had been to her and that she wanted to share.

This woman's example of being willing to sacrifice without any expectations touched me deeply and left me pondering my own sacrifices and expectations. That sister has helped me to fight against feelings of distance from heaven when material desires have not been granted. This woman, like the widow who gave her two mites in the temple (see Mark 12:42), was willing to give all she had with no thought for what she would receive in return. Never once did it enter her mind that she might be the person in need.

## A Miracle Delayed

One of my favorite stories of timing in the scriptures is found in Mark 5, involving Jairus, his dying daughter, and the woman with an issue of blood. The story began with a ruler of the synagogue, named Jairus, who came and fell at Jesus' feet, begging Him to help his daughter, who was on the verge of dying. The next part of the story contains interesting details if read from the viewpoint of Jairus: "And Jesus went with him; and much people followed him, and thronged him" (Mark 5:24). How frustrating it must have been for this panic-stricken father. His young daughter was at the point of death and Jesus had agreed to help, but now multitudes of people were thronging Jesus and slowing their progress.

In that setting, we are introduced to another person, also in need of a miracle—a woman who had suffered with an issue of blood for twelve years. In the first century context, she would have been considered ceremonially unclean for all those years and unable to participate in the normal events of the religious community. She "had suffered many things of many physicians, and had spent all that she had, and was nothing bettered, but rather grew worse" (v. 26). It is easy for us to read her story today and quickly skim over the fact that her struggles had lasted twelve years. But think of where you were twelve years ago to fully appreciate the length of her suffering. Consider what her life had been like during all those years. How distant heaven must have felt on too many sleepless nights! With nowhere else to turn, she heard of Jesus' presence in her village. His name must have kindled great hope among the community of the sick and afflicted. She came pushing through the crowd behind Jesus and touched the hem of His garment. She was immediately healed. Having received what she had so desperately desired, the woman faded back into the crowd.

But Jesus was not finished helping this woman of great faith. He stopped, turned around, and asked, "Who touched my clothes?" (v. 30). Picture this moment from Jairus' perspective, when every second could be the difference between life and death for his daughter. Even the disciples thought Jesus' question a little strange considering the multitude that was crowding Him. The woman was afraid, knowing she had broken multiple societal norms and Law of Moses regulations, but she came forward, fell down, and told Jesus everything that had happened (see v. 33). The Lord took extra time to complete the spiritual aspects of this miracle when He mercifully spoke to her: "Daughter, thy faith hath made thee whole; go in peace, and be whole of thy plague" (v. 34). She had become *clean* by reaching out to Christ, and now she had been made *whole* because He had reached out to her.

*She had become* clean *by reaching out to Christ, and now she had been made* whole *because He had reached out to her.*

What anxiety those added moments and Jesus' perceived lack of urgency must have given Jairus, desperate for a miracle of his own. "While [Jesus] yet spake, there came from the ruler of the synagogue's house certain [people] which said, Thy daughter is dead: why troublest thou the Master any further?" (v. 35). Imagine the flood of emotion that must have swept over Jairus at that moment. All hopes for his daughter's recovery were dashed. Even though he was in Jesus' presence, heaven must have felt distant. But Jesus propped up Jairus' faith with a simple command: "Be not afraid, only believe" (v. 36). Jairus did believe, though all logic would have urged him to be angry or despondent.

Jesus forbade the crowd from following Him but took Jairus and three of His Apostles into the house. He had the mourners removed after they laughed Him to scorn for saying the girl was sleeping. They knew full well she was dead. Jesus then took the young girl by the hand and commanded her to arise from the dead.

In most miracles, Jesus' power is accessed by the faith of the individuals involved in the event. The woman in the street who had suffered for twelve years demonstrated she still had faith by going to great lengths to touch the hem of Jesus' garment. Jairus came on behalf of his daughter and then retained his faith even when he knew his daughter was dead. We also experience situations involving delays and seeming impossibilities. At times like these, we strain to hear with spiritual ears the Savior's reassuring words, "Be not afraid, only believe."

## Prayers over Decades

President Dieter F. Uchtdorf said, "Doubt your doubts before you doubt your faith."[4] Applying this counsel is much easier in short spurts than in prolonged tests of endurance. One of the greatest examples of this is the experience of Abraham and Sarah. They had been promised a numerous posterity, and yet they still had no children when he was one hundred and she was ninety, well past childbearing years. It would have been easy for them to abandon their faith, grow bitter, and mourn the seemingly unfulfilled promise. Certainly, it would have been simpler had the Lord warned them about the delayed timing for the delivery of His promises. Instead, He told them *what* He was going to do but didn't tell them *when* it would happen. When the messengers of God informed Abraham and Sarah that she would conceive and bear a son, she "laughed within herself," knowing the *impossibility* of that promise considering their age (Genesis 18:12). When their son was born, they named him Isaac, which can mean *laughter* in Hebrew.

If getting Isaac to earth had been their most difficult trial of faith, theirs would still be a remarkable story. Abraham and Sarah's greatest test, however, came when God commanded the sacrifice of Isaac. One can only imagine what questions must have swirled through Abraham's mind during the three-day journey from his home to Mount Moriah in Jerusalem. His long-awaited son, and the means whereby the promise of numerous posterity would come true, was now to be slain. Both Abraham and Isaac had the choice to refuse to submit to this command, but both obeyed before ever knowing there would be a happy ending. Thankfully, an angel appeared just in time to prevent Isaac's death. A male lamb was taken from a thicket and replaced Isaac on the altar.

How different Abraham's story would have been had he or Isaac been unwilling to trust the Lord's wisdom, goodness, and promises! Jacob spoke of this sacrifice as a similitude of the Savior's sacrifice (see Jacob 4:5). In contrast, no angel appeared just in time to stop the sacrifice of God's only begotten Son. How different would our story be if Jesus had not completed a perfect Atonement for us (see 2 Nephi 9:7–9)? Both the Father and the Son had roles to play in order for the infinite atoning price to be paid. We understand so little about the actual process of the Atonement, but we know that Heavenly Father and Jesus Christ both fulfilled all that was required for our salvation.

## Perfect Timing

Another who struggled over a long period of time was the widow who was asked by Elijah to exercise tremendous faith (see 1 Kings 17). The famine Elijah had called down had lasted for many years. Even he as the prophet was not immune from its effects. Once the Brook Cherith dried up, the Lord commanded him to go into Zarephath and find a widow to sustain him. At the gate of the city, he saw a woman gathering sticks and asked her to fetch him a little drink of water.

Without questioning she turned to fulfill his request, but she was interrupted when he called after her to also bring him a little morsel of bread. Her response was revealing: "As the Lord thy God liveth, I have not a cake, but an handful of meal in a barrel, and a little oil in a cruse: and, behold, I am gathering two sticks, that I may go in and dress it for me and my son, that we may eat it, and die" (1 Kings 17:12).

If two sticks are any indication of the size of fire necessary to bake the remaining food, we can deduce that this final meal was not going to be much more than a few bites for this mother and her son. We can also safely assume that she had been steadily rationing and cutting portions of food for some time, waiting and hoping for the famine to abate. Both she and her son would have likely been no strangers to the pain of increasing hunger.

With this new information provided to Elijah about her dire condition, Elijah could have rescinded the request and let her eat her last supper in peace with her son. Or better yet, the Lord could have sent Elijah to Zarephath months earlier, when she could have more easily justified sharing some of her precious food with him. Instead, the Lord asked for her sacrifice at the exact moment when it would try this poor widow's faith in the most profound way. It is in such moments that we discover the depth of our commitment to God.

"And Elijah said unto her, Fear not; go and do as thou hast said: but make me thereof a little cake first, and bring it unto me, and after make for thee and for thy son" (v. 13). How peculiar that request must have sounded to the woman. Had Elijah not heard how little food she had left? In essence, he was asking her to make three cakes! I love the faith of this unnamed widow. She trusted in the prophet's promise that the Lord would not allow her supply to fail until the famine ended. She went and did what Elijah asked. Miraculously, they all ate for many days. What the account doesn't tell us is *how* that happened. Did the barrel and cruse miraculously fill once she made the cake for Elijah, or was there always just enough to make one more meal until the famine ended? We don't know. What we do know, however, is that for this widow and her son, the heaven that had seemed so far away became remarkably near through consecrated sacrifice.

*The heaven that had seemed so far away became remarkably near through consecrated sacrifice.*

## Motivation for Obedience

As important as obedience and sacrifice are, our motivation is also critically important. When father Lehi was commanded to depart into the wilderness, there was no hesitation on his part; he quickly obeyed. Laman and Lemuel, on the other hand, sluggishly obeyed. Nephi informed us that his father did as he was commanded because he was an obedient person (see 1 Nephi 2:3). Laman and Lemuel obeyed because "[their] father did speak unto them . . . with power, being filled with the Spirit, until their frames did shake before him. And he did confound them, that they durst not utter against him" (v. 14). Their obedience was driven by fear. This kind of obedience does not create a greater connection with the Lord. In fact, it led to resentment in Laman and Lemuel. They soon got to the point that they could no longer be prodded into submission and became increasingly hard-hearted. Contrastingly, Lehi's motivation for obedience refined him and brought him closer to the Lord.

This is not to say that all submission has to be like Lehi's—swift, decisive, and rooted in appropriate motives. There may be times when, like Laman and Lemuel, we struggle to do the right thing. The key is to continually monitor the intentions of our heart throughout the process and pray for help so our obedience will be consecrated for the welfare of our soul (see 2 Nephi 32:8–9).

## The Moment to Act

When making major life decisions, time and patient effort are both appropriate and helpful. Ammon's approach to missionary service demonstrated this need for patiently serving while waiting for the Lord's will and timing to be fulfilled. Ammon had given up the Nephite throne and was well prepared to be a successful missionary. He had made great sacrifices before he found himself in front of King Lamoni. Despite all his preparation, Ammon perceived that Lamoni was not yet ready to receive the gospel, so he asked to be a servant.

The Book of Mormon account tells us that he had been in the service of the king for three days when the opportunity to defend the king's flocks presented itself (see Alma 17:26). What the book doesn't tell us is what it was like for Ammon to be a lowly servant among the Lamanites for those three days of servitude, when he could have been king of the Nephites. But it seems Ammon gave no heed to possible feelings of self-doubt or regret. He was comfortable with his role, and he waited for the Lord to open doors he couldn't open himself. Ammon's reliance on the Lord's timing rather than his own made all the difference.

*When God's cosmic clock collides with our earthly wristwatch, we must trust that as our all-knowing Father, He can teach us to recognize and follow His guiding hands in both!*

In other situations, the Lord requires quick obedience. This is especially critical when it comes to temptation. Elder Neal A. Maxwell said, "Unlike some of us, [Jesus] did not fantasize, reconsider, or replay temptations. How is it that you and I do not see that while initially we are stronger and the temptations weaker, dalliance turns things upside down?"[5] The longer we allow a temptation to linger, the more likely we are to give in. We are more likely to feel distant from heaven when we delay doing that which we know we should.

When should we wait as Ammon did, and when should we act immediately as counseled by Elder Maxwell? Learning elementary times tables is critical for a student to be able to understand higher principles of mathematics and solve more complicated problems down the road. Learning the *Lord's* time tables and trusting them works the same way. When God's cosmic clock collides with our earthly wristwatch, we must trust that as our all-knowing Father, He can teach us to recognize and follow His guiding hands in both!

CHAPTER 4

# Heavenly Parents, Earthly Children

*"Believe that man doth not comprehend all the things which the Lord can comprehend."*
*—Mosiah 4:9*

God's perfect timing is demonstrated in every interaction He has with His children. Thousands of years ago, the Lord needed someone to represent Him and cry repentance to wicked people. He chose Enoch. In spite of the divine call, Enoch offered the Lord three reasons why he was *not* the right person for the job: "[I] am but a lad [of roughly sixty-five years of age], and all the people hate me; for I am slow of speech; wherefore am I thy servant?" (Moses 6:31).

Note how Enoch stated these limitations as if the Lord did not already know about them. We cannot fathom the idea of the Lord responding by saying, "You're right, Enoch. I was not aware of those constraints. Go back to what you were doing, and I will find someone better qualified." Instead, Enoch received a repeat of the prophetic call followed by a life-changing invitation: "Walk with me" (v. 34).

The next 365 years of preaching taught Enoch how much the Lord could accomplish through a willing instrument. Enoch learned to completely trust the Lord as he was being molded, shaped, and sharpened. The Lord knew Enoch's limitations, but he also knew Enoch's capacity. This experience embodies one of President

Thomas S. Monson's most hope-filled teachings: "Whom the Lord calls, the Lord qualifies."[1]

In many ways, our own stories are similar to Enoch's. Each of us is called upon by the Lord to pass through pain, trials, tribulations, or temptations that seem beyond us. We too can list all the reasons why we are not fit for assisting in God's work. Enoch's example provides comforting perspective as we remember that God does not send us on errands *alone*. Rather, He invites us to walk *with* Him. We lack ability, time, energy, patience, and knowledge, but we can put our trust in the one being who lacks nothing. Jesus is willing to work with us as we grow. However, this personal development cannot occur against our will.

*We lack ability, time, energy, patience, and knowledge, but we can put our trust in the one being who lacks nothing.*

We must submit to God as a child submits to his or her parents. In doing this, we will better recognize what our Heavenly Parents are doing with us as their earthly children as they shape our perspective, fill us with their love, and guide us through our stages of development. In coming to know our Heavenly Parents better, we discover our own identity and find greater motivation to reach for our full potential in the process.

## Avoiding "Overwhelm-ment"

President Dieter F. Uchtdorf said, "You are not alone on this journey. Your Heavenly Father knows you. Even when no one else hears you, He hears you. When you rejoice in righteousness, He rejoices with you. When you are beset with trial, He grieves with you."[2] He went on to explain *why* that is the case: "Heavenly Father's interest in you does not depend on how rich or beautiful or healthy or smart you are. He sees you not as the world sees you; He sees who you really are. He looks on your heart. And He loves you because you are His child."

Even with this knowledge, life's realities combined with the gospel's requirements can become so challenging that we become overwhelmed. My wife, Kiplin, keeps a family journal in which she records the fun, significant, or meaningful experiences we have individually and collectively as a family. In this journal, she shared an insightful perspective on this problem of being overwhelmed:

"I've always told myself to think in terms of the big picture. But sometimes my tendency to do that with some things can get in the way by creating a feeling of 'overwhelm-ment.' The big picture is essential and helps with questions such as: Who am I? Why am I here? Where am I going? But in my day-to-day challenges, the long view can sometimes feel daunting and out of reach. In these moments, instead of focusing on the big picture, I have found value in focusing on the things that are immediately in front of me and acting on them, independent of my past struggles or possible future failures. Taking life one moment at a time, one conversation, one smile, one task, one fear, one apology, one kindness, one hug, and one prayer at a time can ease our feelings of overwhelm-ment. This opens our hearts to the light, love, and hope that comes from our Savior and His role in both our big-picture destiny and the daily details of our strivings to get there."

## Infinite Wisdom

As mortal beings, we often fall into the trap of thinking, *If I do this or that, then God will do such-and-such.* That approach occasionally works out the way we anticipate. But many times, we find out that Isaiah was right when he said that the Lord's thoughts are not our thoughts, neither are our ways His ways, for as the heavens are higher than the earth, so are His ways higher than our ways, and His thoughts higher than our thoughts (see Isaiah 55:8–9).

Consider what would happen if we believed that God lacked infinite perfection. We would treat Him as if He were manning a celestial drive-thru window. With very little effort on our part, we would drive up to the prayer window and place our order by telling Him exactly what we want, how we want it, and when we want it.

Think of how we are tempted to respond when our food is delayed at a restaurant or when a delivery does not match our order. In today's world, we repeatedly hear phrases like, "The customer is always right." This is not true when dealing with the God of the universe. *He* is always right, even when we don't get what we asked for or when it isn't delivered when we wanted. What would become of us if we could dictate every outcome and blessing and control the timing as well? What character traits would we develop in such a one-sided relationship? We would quickly become spiritual spoiled brats if our thoughts, perspectives, and desires overruled God's infinite wisdom.

Thankfully, every desire we have is not quickly and completely fulfilled. God's eternal goal is not great customer service; it is our eternal welfare. He is not a servant whose sole purpose is to meet our demands and desires. He does not want to extricate us from every possible trial, hurt, or difficult situation that may arise. He knows it is these very experiences that help refine us and provide great opportunities to reach our eternal potential. God loves *us* more than He loves our tranquility. Because of this, He will not deprive us of shaping influences, despite how frustrating they may seem at the moment.

*Thankfully, every desire we have is not quickly and completely fulfilled. God's eternal goal is not great customer service; it is our eternal welfare.*

## Ask with Perspective

There is nothing wrong with making requests of God; in fact, we have been commanded to ask, seek, and knock. Feelings of a distant heaven often come not from having requests but from having unrealistic or false expectations regarding what God's response to our requests should be. Some of life's greatest periods of personal growth come when our prayers appear to go unheard and unanswered. We stretch. We reach. We plead. We cling to hope. But most of all, we hold fast to the belief that God has our best interest in mind, even though we may not understand. We simply accept the fact that our perspective is greatly limited, while His is limitless and eternal.

*Only with the Lord's help can we grow through trials rather than just go through them.*

The Lord informed Joseph Smith and other early members of the Church, "Ye are little children and ye cannot bear all things now; ye must grow in grace and in the knowledge of the truth" (D&C 50:40). It is often when heaven feels most distant, in our darkest hours, that our hope and childlike trust have the most impact. Only with the Lord's help can we *grow* through trials rather than just *go* through them.

## Real Love

History's heroes were intimately acquainted with intense pain, difficulty, and opposition. Could some of these heart-wrenching struggles actually be a sign of God's great love rather than a manifestation of His neglect? This concept becomes easier to understand if we observe earthly parenting techniques and consider possible similarities to Heavenly Parenting methods.

My wife and I have experienced the wails of frustration from all our babies as we have removed choking hazards from their hands and mouths—objects that they *really wanted* but that could have proven fatal. We have listened to many complaints from our children of all ages about having to eat the healthy parts of a meal rather than being allowed to fill up on desserts and junk food. We have endured the momentary cries of pain as cuts, scrapes, and slivers have been properly treated to allow for complete recovery. This perceived unkindness also includes setting up gates to prevent little babies from falling down stairs or crawling into places where they are likely to get hurt.

These necessary restrictions and denials are the benevolent boundaries that keep our children safe, healthy, and ultimately happy. The child, however, does not see it this way. Surely we can see ourselves in each of these scenarios.

Moms and dads recognize that little children, if left to do what they want, will not grow up to reach their full potential. Therefore, parents, acting out of love, do their best to act for the ultimate safety, happiness, and development of the child. This disconnect between parental wisdom and a child's limited perspective is especially obvious when it comes time for immunizations. Can we recognize ourselves and our Heavenly Parents in that scenario? As we hold our screaming child, his or her entire focus is on the needles and the pain. In that same moment, our full attention is focused on the child. Yet the child seems unaware of our calming efforts because of the pain and fear of the moment. Though the hurt from those shots is real, it passes quickly, leaving us inoculated and protected from much more serious consequences in the future.

*I believe it is precisely at the most painful times, when heaven feels most distant, that our loving Heavenly Parents are actually closest to us.*

Oddly, as is the case with children getting immunized, it is in our most painful moments that we seem the least aware of our Parents' presence and what They are doing to reassure us. I believe it is precisely at the most painful times, when heaven feels most distant, that our loving Heavenly Parents are actually closest to us.

## Never Alone?

Feeling close to heaven is possible because of the infinite price Jesus paid for our redemption. During His ministry, Jesus said, "He that sent me is with me: *the Father hath not left me alone*; for I do always those things that please him" (John 8:29; emphasis added). He reiterated the closeness He felt with His Father in Heaven right before entering Gethsemane, when He informed His Apostles that they would "be scattered, every man to his own, and shall leave me alone" (John 16:32). Even knowing they would all abandon Him, Jesus held fast to His most treasured feeling of connectedness: "And yet I am not alone, because the Father is with me."

We could logically assume that at that critical moment, the Father would never have had more reason to be close to His Son. Based on the scriptural account, however, it appears that Jesus soon felt utterly and completely cut off from that divine presence. It was from the cross the next day that Jesus uttered the soul-wrenching cry, "My God, my God, why hast *thou* forsaken me?" (Mark 15:34; emphasis added).

*He who knows infinitely well what it feels like to suffer in complete isolation promises that He will never leave us alone.*

Before Jesus could ultimately say, "It is finished" (John 19:30), He had to "[tread] the wine-press alone, even the wine-press of the fierceness of the wrath of Almighty God" (D&C 76:107) to pay the debt of sin for all of God's children. Referencing that crucial moment on the cross, Elder Jeffrey R. Holland has said, "It is my personal belief that in all of Christ's mortal ministry the Father may never have been closer to His Son than in these agonizing final moments of suffering." He went on to explain, "It was required, indeed it was central to the significance of the Atonement, that this perfect Son who had never spoken ill nor done wrong . . . had to feel . . . what it was like to have the divine Spirit withdraw, leaving one feeling totally, abjectly, hopelessly alone."[3] He who knows infinitely well what it feels like to suffer in complete isolation promises that He will never leave us alone (see John 14:18).

## Hesitant to Confident

Our journey through mortality can be compared to a young child learning to walk. Initially, parents grip their child's fingers tightly with hands-on guidance and encouragement. Soon they pull back, not because they want to see the baby fall, but because she cannot progress further until they allow her to experience walking and falling on her own. Parents quickly come to her aid when she stumbles and falls, but somewhere along the way, wise parents know when to stop rushing to the rescue. This is not because they *can't* help but rather because it is no longer helpful. The toddler may think, *Why won't they help? I have tried so hard. I've done everything I can, and now they have abandoned me.* What the parents understand is that it is necessary to allow the child to wrestle through the process of taking uncertain and shaky steps in order to gain the necessary confidence to walk—and eventually run.

This is similar to our spiritual development. As our abilities increase, our confidence in ourselves and in the Lord also grows. It is when we perceive ourselves as being forsaken that our growth is often the greatest.

As capability grows, confidence increases. We see this same pattern in the Church's development over time. As an example of this, the frequency of revelations recorded in the Doctrine and Covenants decreased as the Church matured. More recently, missionaries have been given more responsibility to follow the Spirit in their teaching rather than delivering memorized lessons. This requires greater reliance on the Lord and more confidence in their ability to learn and teach the gospel. In *Come, Follow Me,* our youth are taught correct principles and then asked to prayerfully consider how to apply them. They are no longer given long lists of rigid dos and don'ts. Teachers in the Church are asked to rely on the Lord as they meet the needs of their students, rather than robotically delivering lesson material from prepackaged manuals.

This is not meant to imply that the Lord will stop giving guidance and direction after a certain point of spiritual maturity. The reality is quite the opposite. Direction still comes, just differently than we often anticipate. As we grow in the gospel, we should expect, like the struggling yet developing toddler, to wrestle with challenges, find our footing, and discover that we actually have the capacity to stand up and make our way through uncharted territory. These situations are opportunities for growth as the divine potential within us reaches out, struggles, matures, and then discovers new knowledge, abilities, and confidence.

*These situations are opportunities for growth as the divine potential within us reaches out, struggles, matures, and then discovers new knowledge, abilities, and confidence.*

## The Power of True Identity

In preparing Moses for the challenge of confronting Pharaoh and then spending forty years wandering in the wilderness, God gave him a much-needed perspective regarding his true identity. Moses was caught up into an exceedingly high mountain and transfigured so he could endure God's divine presence (see Moses 1:1–2). Imagine how he must have felt standing face to face with God, hearing these words,

"Behold, I am the Lord God Almighty, and Endless is my name; for I am without beginning of days or end of years; and is not this endless?" (v. 3). Surely this grand introduction evoked feelings of utter inadequacy in Moses. The next statement, however, changed everything: "And, behold, *thou art my son*" (v. 4; emphasis added).

Children have a propensity to become like their parents. Keeping that in mind allows us to see God's three-verse introduction as much more than a description of His own perfected attributes; it is a revelation of what Moses and all of us can *become*. President Boyd K. Packer taught, "Spiritually you are of noble birth, the offspring of the King of Heaven . . . no matter what race or people you represent, the pedigree of your spirit can be written on a single line. You are a child of God!"[4]

When we understand our own true identity, we are more capable of seeing our children and others from that same perspective as well. When my wife and I took Benjamin, our oldest son, to the airport to fly to the Guatemala Missionary Training Center, I couldn't have been happier for him. This was exactly what I wanted for his life. So why did my heart hurt so deeply? Why did I already miss him so profoundly as I watched him go through the security checkpoint? Based on my own mission experience in Brazil many years ago, I knew he was going to learn priceless lessons. I knew he would touch many lives and be touched by countless people in return. But that knowledge did not prevent my tears from flowing freely, nor did it explain the ache that welled up in my heart that day.

*When we understand our own true identity, we are more capable of seeing our children and others from that same perspective as well.*

This was our son! Heavenly Parents had given him to us, and now we were symbolically giving him back to them. As he turned and waved one more time before disappearing down the terminal, an understanding of our Heavenly Parents' love for each of us became more *real.* We marveled at the supernal privilege we had been granted to be a part of Benjamin's development and growth. Even so, this perspective and knowledge did not magically remove the heartache of saying goodbye.

I remember with clarity the day he was born. He didn't graciously turn to my wife and thank her for putting up with the extreme discomfort of pregnancy followed by the pain of labor and delivery. He didn't thank us for the cost and effort to get him safely delivered. He never expressed concern for disturbing our sleep at all hours of the night to feed, change, or help him through painful bouts of colic. But as new parents, we felt that Benjamin was the most amazing thing to ever happen to us, and we loved him immediately and completely.

An understanding of eternal identity helps mothers and fathers marvel at the miracle of creating new life rather than focusing on the discomforts and inconveniences of parenthood. They gratefully wrap their hearts and lives around their little ones. We love that for which we sacrifice; the greater the sacrifice, the greater the potential for love. This is especially true of our Heavenly Parents' interactions with us. "We love [them], because [they] first loved us" (1 John 4:19). Parents love children not because of what they get *out* of them but because of what they put *into* them! Understanding this principle helps us begin to comprehend why our Heavenly Parents love us so perfectly.

*Parents love children not because of what they get* out *of them but because of what they put* into *them!*

CHAPTER 5

# Moving Forward Despite Ambiguity

*"I would not give a fig for the simplicity on this side of complexity, but I would give my life for the simplicity on the other side of complexity."*
*—Oliver Wendell Holmes*

Because we are imperfect yet developing children of Heavenly Parents, it is understandable that God would often withhold many answers to our questions until we have the needed context to comprehend the truth. We all know those feelings of uncertainty when our way forward is not clearly marked or well defined. As frustrating as these experiences may be, they often teach us some of life's greatest lessons.

Ambiguity encompasses all situations that are unclear or vague and concepts that can be interpreted in multiple ways. It can be manifest in incomplete instructions from the Lord. It also surfaces when we receive clear instructions that seem to contradict previous directions. When ambiguity is intense, it can create feelings of disconnection from heaven. This can be especially true when wrestling with confusing doctrines, facing troubling historical issues, navigating cultural norms, confronting complex questions, or making major decisions.

Ironically, many of us get frustrated with the Lord when He doesn't make everything clear by telling us exactly what to do. We often marvel at the number of choices we have to make seemingly stepping forward into the darkness, relying on faith alone. The irony lies in the fact that we fought for our agency before coming to this earth, and we won! But now we feel shortchanged when God gives us the very thing we fought for—freedom to think, feel, and act "according to the dictates of our own conscience" (Article of Faith 11). It's as if we are saying to Him, "Never mind. I don't want this kind of freedom after all. Just tell me what to do and I will do it."

*We fought for our agency before coming to this earth, and we won! But now we feel shortchanged when God gives us the very thing we fought for—freedom to think, feel, and act "according to the dictates of our own conscience."*

To help us turn these potential frustrations into growth opportunities, Sister Virginia H. Pearce has recommended four considerations: "(1) Rejoice in ambiguity and expect revelation, (2) Review the certainties, (3) Slow down—Grappling with ambiguity takes time and energy, and (4) Carve out regular quiet spaces and places in everyday life to just think and be still." Sister Pearce explained, "Ambiguity is a cause for celebration because over and over it invites us to seek revelation from God. . . . When we receive personal revelation by which to make life choices, we are far less likely to look at the lives of others and envy them—or worse still, look at the lives of others and criticize their choices."[1]

Sister Pearce concluded her thoughts with a quote from her father, President Gordon B. Hinckley, who taught, "You need time to meditate and ponder, to think, to wonder at the great plan of happiness that the Lord has outlined for His children. . . . Our lives become extremely busy. We run from one thing to another. . . . We are entitled to spend some time with ourselves in introspection, in development. . . . Your needs and your tastes along these lines will vary with your age. But all of us need some of it."[2]

Clearly, the Lord has not left us without resources for seeking answers to our questions and uncertainties. God has inspired the invention of powerful tools such as the Internet and other new methods for discovering truths of all kinds. Unfortunately, there are so many voices claiming authority in the world that finding real truth can be challenging. Fortunately, the Lord provides spiritual discernment and guidance for those who earnestly seek to know His will by encouraging them to seek eternal truth through valid and reliable sources. By anchoring our faith in the Lord and nothing else, we will better know how to address difficult issues that might otherwise weaken our faith, encourage us to seek truth in the wrong places, or adopt false expectations regarding God.

## Truth in the Information Age

Whatever the source or form of ambiguity, a quick overview of the scriptures reveals that uncertainty is one of the Lord's most effective instruments for shaping character and building faith. Some members of the Church experience feelings of frustration and distance from the Lord when they discover something unsettling about Church history or doctrine. When our previously firm foundation begins to feel like shaky ground, we instinctively reach out for something to steady us. We want to know the *truth.* We want feelings of peace to return to our hearts. We want to make sense of our situation and standing before God. Unfortunately, the answers we seek are often not easy to find or simple to understand. Finding equilibrium can be a messy and slow process that only unfolds over time through diligent effort.

Part of the problem lies in the fact that we don't always look in the right places for the most important answers. A colleague at the Logan Institute, Tom Cherrington, shared an insight with me years ago when he jokingly said that there surely must be a scripture somewhere in hell that reads, "If any of ye lack wisdom, let him ask of Google." This is not to say that the Internet is evil. It was clearly inspired to increase the quality of life for God's children and to help bring about His purposes. For matters of earthly importance, the Internet is a wonderful resource for sharing information. Problems arise, however, when we use the combined wisdom of the world as a replacement for God when seeking answers to questions with eternal consequences.

The growth of the Internet has increased our opportunities for finding truth, but it has also increased our likelihood of finding divergent opinions on nearly every topic. In this worldwide web of information, anyone can be portrayed as a prophet, historian, or authoritative expert on nearly any subject, including what is morally right and wrong, true or false, acceptable or not. This difficult reality, however, does not minimize the importance of researching to gain understanding. On the contrary, it maximizes it. Joseph Smith went through a long study process before he experienced his First Vision (see JS—History 1:11–13). Contrast this with Oliver Cowdery, who attempted to receive revelation quickly and effortlessly, without properly preparing. The Lord reprimanded him by saying, "Behold, you have not understood; you have supposed that I would give it unto you, when you took no thought save it was to ask me" (D&C 9:7).

*The growth of the Internet has increased our opportunities for finding truth, but it has also increased our likelihood of finding divergent opinions on nearly every topic.*

Elder Dallin H. Oaks explained that there are two ways of gaining knowledge: the spiritual and the scientific methods. He clarified that these two are not in conflict with each other "because God, our omnipotent Eternal Father, knows all truth and beckons us to learn by them both."[3]

Increased exposure to conflicting philosophies and ideologies is not the lone source of growing uncertainty in our world. Another cause is difficulty in identifying God's authorized channels of truth amid a sea of variant voices. Most people don't lose their faith by spending too much time in the scriptures and the words of the prophets. But many get there by ignoring the words of the Lord and spending too much time seeking the opinions of the world's "experts." Nephi saw that a major problem in our day would be "[hearkening] unto the precepts of men, and [denying] the power of God, and the gift of the Holy Ghost" (2 Nephi 28:26). Seeing our day through the prophetic corridors of time, Nephi wrote, "Cursed is he that putteth his trust in man, or maketh flesh his arm, or shall hearken unto the precepts of men, save their precepts shall be given by the power of the Holy Ghost" (2 Nephi 28:31).

## Vertical and Horizontal Sources

This contrast between heavenly and earthly sources of truth is illustrated by the multitude in 3 Nephi 11 who gathered at the temple after the great destruction in the Americas. The first time the crowd heard Heavenly Father's voice, they "cast their eyes round about" (3 Nephi 11:3). They were looking *horizontally* to make sense of something they were receiving *vertically.*[4] Each person in the crowd was just as confused as everyone else, so those horizontal looks did nothing to enlighten anyone. This occurred a second time with the same result. The people made an adjustment the third time by opening their ears to hear and looking toward heaven (v. 5). By looking vertically for clarity and answers rather than horizontally, they were able to understand the voice of the Father.

*Horizontal sources of spiritual information are not created equally.*

Horizontal sources of spiritual information are not created equally. They seem to fall somewhere on a scale from factual and helpful to manipulative and evil. A major need in this answers-at-our-fingertips age is to evaluate not only what is being promoted but also who is presenting the information and what authority for truth they have. To illustrate this point, pretend you are given the assignment to pick two people from the following descriptions to recommend for important callings in your ward or stake:

**Person 1:** His father is a prominent Church leader. He rebelled in his youth and refused to serve a mission at that time. He has since shown full repentance and has proven to be a faithful disciple who has served faithfully for many years now.

**Person 2:** His father is also a prominent Church leader. He is willing to sacrifice and occasionally has direct communication with the Lord. He is a successful farmer.

**Person 3:** He is very short, moves frequently, and is a recent convert to the Church. Many members of your stake do not trust him due to his problematic past. He often makes people angry because he questions traditional practices and authority.

**Person 4:** He demonstrates powerful leadership abilities and is ambitious and hard-working. He is good at discerning other's strengths and weaknesses. He has tremendous amounts of knowledge, comes from an excellent family, and is very persuasive.

**Person 5:** He has developed into a great writer and speaker over the years. He is charismatic, but many people think he is deceptive. Even though he has spent many months in prison, he is now out. He still causes occasional riots and unrest. School was not really his strength.

Based on those descriptions, which two did you pick? Person 1, with the rebellious youth, was Alma the Younger, one of the greatest prophets of the Book of Mormon. Person 2 is Cain, who slew Abel. Person 3, not likely to be selected by most readers, was Paul, previously

Saul of Tarsus. Person 4 is likely to garner many votes; ironically, that was Lucifer himself. Person 5 is the Prophet Joseph Smith.

## SEEDs of Discernment

Notice how easy it was to make good appear evil and evil appear good (see 2 Nephi 15:20). Our world twists facts in one direction or the other or withholds certain details to try to prove or disprove a point. But we are not left defenseless or without resource in our search for truth. Jesus gave us a key when He said, "By their fruits ye shall know them" (Matthew 7:20). Good horizontal sources seek to connect us with vertical sources and leave us feeling the fruits of faith, hope, and charity. Destructive horizontal sources mock vertical sources, sowing weeds of doubt, hopelessness, confusion, emptiness, and contention.

*Good horizontal sources seek to connect us with vertical sources and leave us feeling the fruits of faith, hope, and charity.*

Alma gave us an instructive analogy to use when seeking truth by comparing the words we hear to a seed (see Alma 32:28). He proposed we plant these seeds in our heart. He assured us that if they are good, they will do four things that form a memorable acronym:

**S**–Swell within our hearts
**E**–Enlarge our souls
**E**–Enlighten our understanding
**D**–Delicious to us

I never experience a swelling, enlarging, enlightening, *or* delicious experience when I read material that seeks to destroy faith. I feel deflated, empty, and confused and am left with a bad taste. When I turn to the Lord's sources of truth, however, I feel a noticeable difference, both spiritually and physiologically. I become calmer, more peaceful, more willing to keep the commandments, and more motivated to turn outward and serve others, and I feel more connected with heaven. Growing good seeds takes time and diligent effort before we can partake of the fruit that grows in its season.

## Validity and Reliability

To illustrate the importance of source checking, consider the following three scenarios. Evaluate how well you could rely on information gained from each of these sources:

What would you likely hear if you asked a business owner to tell you about one of his or her competitors?

When marriages or relationships end on bitter terms, what would you learn if you asked both parties to describe their ex-spouse?

What would you learn about Jesus of Nazareth by interviewing Pharisees and Sadducees from the First Century?

As illustrated in these examples, competitors, estranged or embittered associates, or enemies are rarely reliable sources of truth. In fact, their words usually reveal more about themselves than about the person they are describing.

Happily, we have many horizontal sources that align with vertical sources. These can include prophets, spouses, parents, grandparents, children, other relations, ward and stake leaders, teachers, and true friends. These sources of truth are not perfect, but their concern for our eternal well-being sets them apart.

Unfortunately, we can find examples of times when some of these trusted sources of truth behave or speak imperfectly. When this involves Church leaders, detractors use this as "evidence" that the Church can't be true. Using this same logic, we could walk into a math class and point out instances where a teacher has not adequately explained an important concept or where students have made mistakes on their assignments. This would not be good evidence that *math* is flawed. In the same way, the value of the gospel cannot be determined by a person's imperfection in teaching or following its principles; it is manifest whenever a person *correctly* applies its teachings and ordinances. Everyone but Jesus has fallen short of correctly applying the principles of the gospel at one time or another. Gratefully, we don't go to church to celebrate *our* perfection; we go to celebrate *Christ's* perfection and to plead for His help.

*Gratefully, we don't go to church to celebrate* our *perfection; we go to celebrate* Christ's *perfection and to plead for His help.*

## Incomplete Instructions

Dealing with partial instructions can also cause feelings of ambiguity and distance from heaven. In the beginning, the Lord commanded Adam and Eve to "offer the firstlings of their flocks, for an offering unto the Lord. And Adam was obedient unto the commandments of the Lord" (Moses 5:5). Regarding those earliest sacrifices, Adam and Eve knew two things, *what* to do and *how* to do it, but they didn't know *why*.[5] After many days, an angel appeared to Adam and asked, "Why dost thou offer sacrifices unto the Lord? And Adam said unto him: I know not, save the Lord commanded me" (v. 6). Adam and Eve did not allow ambiguity or uncertainty to overpower what they knew for certain—God had commanded them to sacrifice, and they obeyed. At the outset, they had no guarantee that they would ever learn the *why*. Thus, we clearly see their demonstration of faith despite ambiguity. In time, Adam and Eve learned about the symbolic connection with the ultimate sacrifice of the Only Begotten of the Father.

Similarly, God told Lehi to send his sons to get the brass plates from Laban. His sons knew *what* to do, and basic reasons for *why* to do it, but they didn't know *how* to get them. Whereas Adam and Eve struggled to know the *why*, these brothers were wrestling with the *how*.

After Laman's first attempt failed, they offered to buy the plates with their father's riches. When that failed, they could have easily given up and returned to Lehi's tent, as Laman and Lemuel suggested. Nephi, however, obediently persisted and went forward into the dark night, being "led by the Spirit, not knowing beforehand the things which [he] should do" (1 Nephi 4:6).

As Nephi proceeded into the darkness of the night, the Lord finally revealed *how* to get the plates. This answer included killing Laban and introduced a much more serious and complex question for Nephi—*why* would the Lord require him to take a life? This command ran contrary to everything he had ever been taught. From this experience, we see that sometimes the answer to one question illuminates our path for one more step, but it also reveals new questions requiring us to exercise faith at a different level.

*Sometimes the answer to one question illuminates our path for one more step, but it also reveals new questions requiring us to exercise faith at a different level.*

Mary, the mother of Jesus, also demonstrated great faith in the face of ambiguity. The angel Gabriel informed her that she had "found favor with God. And, behold, thou shalt conceive in thy womb, and bring forth a son, and shalt call his name Jesus" (Luke 1:30–31). She was told *what* would happen, but she didn't know either the *why* or the *how.* Faced with more questions than certainty, Mary submitted in faith, "Behold the handmaid of the Lord; be it unto me according to thy word" (v. 38). Through this experience, Mary foreshadowed her own firstborn Son—because she was so highly favored of God, she became "despised and rejected of men." Those who knew of her betrothal to Joseph and subsequent untimely pregnancy would never have understood any explanations she could offer, so "Mary kept all these things, and pondered them in her heart" (Luke

2:19). The world's judgment and condemnation was manifest against her when the time came to deliver her baby in Bethlehem, their native city, surrounded by their extended family, and yet, "There was no room for them in the *inns*" (v. 7, JST emphasized).

According to the Greek word, these inns were not what we would think of as motels. They were large common rooms in homes and could be used for large group gatherings. The same Greek word was translated as "upper room" when Jesus ate His last supper with the disciples (Mark 14:15; Luke 22:12). Under normal circumstances, any woman, especially a relative, would make whatever arrangements were necessary to help a fellow woman in labor. But such was not the case on the night of Jesus' birth. Mary's story teaches us that at times, we come to know the answers to some of our deepest questions, but we are not able to adequately share what we know so that others will understand. Rejected by the world, Mary and Joseph were relegated to a lowly stable, where the Creator of worlds without number entered our world. Jesus and his mother were favored of God but rejected of the world.

Like Adam, Nephi, Mary, and many other scripture heroes, we must also wrestle with ambiguity. Rarely does God give clear and complete answers to all questions of *who, what, when, where, how,* and *why* when He first delivers a call. He waits for us to move forward in faith, based on the incomplete instructions He has already given us, for we "receive no witness until *after* the trial of [our] faith" (Ether 12:6; emphasis added). The Lord affirmed the incremental nature of answers and blessings when He said, "Unto him that receiveth it shall be given more abundantly, even power" (D&C 71:6). Consider what the people in each of the following examples know and what they *don't* know:

> A mother feels unsettled about allowing her child to attend a certain event but can't provide a better reason than, "I just don't feel good about this."

> A husband and wife feel inspired that the Lord wants them to welcome a child into their family, but they are struggling to make ends meet on a limited income.
>
> A person feels that the Lord wants him to go to the temple soon, but he already has a full schedule that week.
>
> A student is directed by the Holy Ghost to apply to a certain college, but she knows she is not qualified and will likely be rejected.
>
> Two missionaries both get the prompting to turn around and walk in the opposite direction even though there seems to be no danger ahead.
>
> A bishopric is inspired to call a certain individual to a calling when others in the ward are far more qualified.
>
> A ward member feels prompted to take a meal or reach out to a specific family even though everything seems to be fine with them.

Ambiguous situations such as these force us to trust the promptings of the Spirit and proceed with faith. These people may not know *where* each inspired path may take them, but they know whose path it is.

## Where Should We Go?

A series of events during Paul's second mission shows that even when we think we have a clear direction, the Lord may still insert ambiguity. In the opening of Acts chapter 16, Paul and his companions were confidently traveling toward the province of Asia when the Holy Ghost forbade them from continuing in that direction. So Paul decided to go toward Bithynia instead, "but the Spirit suffered them not" (v. 7). Being stopped twice, Paul decided to turn west toward Troas. Up to this point, the Lord had not told them where to go; He just told them where not to go. It was not until they arrived at the coast that the Lord finally gave Paul a vision wherein he was told to cross the Aegean Sea into Macedonia. Once in Greece, the ambiguity didn't end. Nobody joined the Church in the first few cities they visited. After many days, they finally found success in Philippi with Lydia, their first convert (see v. 14–15).

President Howard W. Hunter said, "Where one door closes, another opens. Doors close regularly in our lives, and some of those closings cause genuine pain and heartache. But I do believe that where one such door closes, another opens (and perhaps more than one), with hope and blessings in other areas of our lives that we might not have discovered otherwise."[6] For Paul, that new door opened so he could commence the work of the gospel in Europe.

What would have happened if Adam had refused to offer a sacrifice until the Lord clarified why it was required? What if Nephi had sat down just inside the wall of Jerusalem, unwilling to move forward until the Lord delivered Laban and the brass plates into his hands? What if Paul would have insisted on a direct answer before proceeding after being stopped on two occasions by the Spirit? The greater the uncertainty we overcome, the greater the triumph of faith and growth of character we experience. Although we cannot always find the answers we desperately want, we *can* proceed in faith, based on what we *do* know. It is easier for God to direct our path when we are moving forward than when we are sitting around, waiting for Him to tell us what to do.

*It is easier for God to direct our path when we are moving forward than when we are sitting around, waiting for Him to tell us what to do.*

## Contradictions and Inconsistencies

Struggles with ambiguity are accentuated when seemingly inconsistent or contradictory statements appear in the scriptures. For instance, during His life, Jesus focused His ministry on the descendants of Israel. He altered that policy on the Mount of Ascension, when He commanded the eleven Apostles to go "into *all* the world, and preach the gospel to *every* creature" (Mark 16:15; emphasis added). This new direction was largely misunderstood or ignored by the Apostles for a few years. The Lord brought about the first Gentile baptisms by giving complementary visions to Peter, the chief Apostle, and Cornelius, a Roman centurion (see Acts 10). Peter's visions on that occasion directly contradicted Israel's strict dietary laws (see Deuteronomy 14). Peter was commanded to kill and eat the very things the Lord had expressly forbidden for 1500 years (see Acts 10:9–17). These policy changes caused anxiety and confusion for some of the Church members in Peter's day.

One trend that emerges from apparent scriptural incongruities is that when the Lord establishes patterns or rules, he sometimes commands exceptions in order for His work to progress—hence the need for living oracles, ongoing revelation, and adaptable practices in the Church. Jesus provided a key for understanding conflicting commandments when He said, "Except ye shall keep my commandments, *which I have commanded you at this time*, ye shall in no case enter into the kingdom of heaven" (3 Nephi 12:20; emphasis added). Changes in policy, practice, and procedure in the Church of Jesus Christ are evidence it is a *living*, growing church.

*Changes in policy, practice, and procedure in the Church of Jesus Christ are evidence it is a* living, *growing church.*

## Differing Interpretations

Another source of distance-inducing ambiguity comes from not fully understanding the Lord's directions or misapplying one of His teachings. To illustrate: Jesus delivered a sermon filled with symbolism that caused many of His disciples to stop following Him at a high point of His popularity (see John 6:26–71). It must have been shocking and troubling to hear Him use phrases such as, "I am the living bread . . . and the bread that I will give is my flesh" (v. 51); "Except ye eat the flesh of the Son of man, and drink his blood, ye have no life in you" (53); or "He that eateth my flesh, and drinketh my blood, dwelleth in me, and I in him" (v. 56). Many of Jesus' followers could not understand and walked away in exasperation (see v. 66). It is intriguing that He did not call them back and explain that the Bread of Life sermon was a symbolic reference to a future ordinance He would call the sacrament. He simply let them walk away without adding clarity or explanation. He then asked His Apostles, "Will ye also go away?" (v. 67). Devoted disciples then and now resonate with Simon Peter's answer: "Lord, to whom shall we go? thou hast the words of eternal life" (v. 68).

Examples of confusion or misapplication of principles or practices are not limited to ancient scripture. For instance, when the revelation came regarding baptisms for the dead, many early Saints excitedly began performing them in the Mississippi River with no semblance of order or recorder present. The Lord did not condemn them for performing the ordinances incorrectly; they had simply done the best they could based on the knowledge they had at that time. Further direction regarding how to properly perform the ordinance soon came through the prophet.

For many today, a particularly troubling practice in Church history is plural marriage. Detractors of the Church can easily paint these situations in the worst possible light by using twenty-first-century lenses to judge what we read from nineteenth-century sources. Joseph had no how-to handbook when it came to implementing the practice. The Lord gave him a command to live the Biblical law of plural marriage, and not unlike Nephi with the brass plates, Joseph had to figure out the *how* along the way.

In a powerful talk reminding us that faith is a choice, Elder Neil L. Andersen gave some advice regarding what to do when we are tempted to condemn Joseph based on our limited understanding of events in those early days: "For now, give Brother Joseph a break! In a future day, you will have 100 times more information than from all of today's search engines combined, and it will come from our all-knowing Father in Heaven."[7] Whether doctrinal clarifications or policy changes come early or late, quickly or slowly, they come according to the Lord's timing when the work requires them and when the people are capable of making needed adjustments.

## Faith in Christ and Nothing Else

The Church is increasingly being held hostage by detractors using everything that has ever been said or done by all leaders throughout its history to highlight incongruities. Ignoring the fruits of discipleship, the world's wisdom today boldly declares, "By their *roots* ye shall know them." We have no control over what happened in the past. We don't know all that will happen in the future. *Our* test of faith lies in the present, in how we respond to the current prophets, practices, and revelations. In an ever-changing world, our faith must be built on Jesus Christ alone, not past quotes, policies, programs, or people.

*We have no control over what happened in the past. We don't know all that will happen in the future.* Our *test of faith lies in the present, in how we respond to the current prophets, practices, and revelations.*

We also distance ourselves from heaven and set ourselves up for failure when we try to dogmatically define that which the Lord has intentionally left as a "gray area" for each to wrestle with on his or her own. Over-zealousness can easily lead to judging others who do not accept or live up to our self-created standards. This is often manifest in extreme or pet practices in areas such as Sabbath observance, the Word of Wisdom, politics, media usage, or activity in a variety of Church-related activities or programs. It is expected that disciples of Christ will set standards for themselves within all of these areas. Problems arise, however, when we hold others accountable to our personal standards and condemn them when they fall short of living "according to the dictates of *our* own conscience" (Article of Faith 11; emphasis added).

## Korihor's Doctrinal Dominoes

One of the great scriptural examples of a detractor spreading doubt and confusion is when Korihor confronted Alma the Younger and attacked the main aspects of the gospel of Jesus Christ. He sought to knock them down like dominoes, one after another. It is not surprising that he began by focusing on the most important doctrine of all, confidently declaring, "There should be no Christ" (Alma 30:12). His next two targets were the people's hope for a brighter future and their belief in the prophecies they had received. Consider who actually embodies Korihor's teachings up to that point. Who has (1) no claim on Christ, (2) no hope for a brighter future, and (3) no access to prophecy or revelation? The devil and his angels are the only ones that fit this description.

This suggests that Korihor's teachings are much more than an arbitrary list of attacks on belief and faith; they essentially reveal the true identity of devils. We don't have to wonder what it is like for them to live in a realm of complete spiritual darkness with no hope for anything good in the future. Korihor's teachings give us a fairly good description of their bleak and miserable existence. The Lord's teachings do the same thing. When the Lord reveals His gospel to us, He is not making up random doctrines and rituals to fill our time or keep us busy; He is revealing aspects of His existence and character to us.

Korihor's attack on doctrine continued with teaching that there is no remission of sins, no Atonement, no spiritual reward, and no life after death. Once again, all of these conditions describe the devils who are seeking that all men might be as miserable as they are (see 2 Nephi 2:27).

*The antidote to the devilish claims of no Christ, no hope, and no prophecy is to* know *Christ,* know *hope, and* know *prophecy.*

The antidote to the devilish claims of no Christ, no hope, and no prophecy is to *know* Christ, *know* hope, and *know* prophecy. In turn, we will *know* all the other truths Korihor sought to tear down. Like a line of dominoes, faith is much easier to destroy than to build up. Many years of testimony building can crumble in a hurry if we allow the devil's efforts to start toppling what we have built.

## Burden of Proof

Those who seek to destroy belief in God use devilish tactics. One of those techniques is to boldly declare, "If you can't answer *all* of my questions, then I won't accept *any* of your answers." Detractors would seek to define us by what we *don't* know rather than what we *do* know. They want us to believe that the question marks in our mind are more valid than the exclamation marks in our hearts. Elder M. Russell Ballard reminded us, "Sometimes we can learn, study, and know, and sometimes we have to believe, trust and hope."[8]

Even though the nonexistence of God cannot be proven by nonbelievers, the devilish tactic is to place the burden of proof on *believers*. Elder Gerald N. Lund explained that proving God's nonexistence would require a person to explore every cubic meter of the vast expanse of the universe and find no trace of God.[9] The trouble is, God can move. Therefore, a person would have to see the entire universe in an instant, which is something only a God can do. God's existence or nonexistence is not something He intended to be proven; He purposely has made it a matter of faith. Alma's testimony was not enough for Korihor. He still demanded a sign before he would believe.

## Sign-Seeking

Jesus taught, "A wicked and adulterous generation seeketh after a sign" (Matthew 16:4). Sign-seekers want all the desired outcomes without having to do the prerequisite work. They try to take what they are seeking from another person rather than earning it for themselves. Korihor's sign-seeking bypasses the process of scripture study, prayer, fasting, and experimenting upon the words of Christ in order to learn truth and believe. He would rather have Alma do all the work and show him a sign, which he could then accept or reject with minimal effort.

The Lord gave Korihor a sign by striking him dumb. Sadly, Korihor still didn't turn to God; he turned to Alma. Once again, he wanted Alma to do all the work of taking away his newly acquired disability. This story would likely have had a different ending if Korihor had pled with the Lord for forgiveness and direction on how to set his life in order. The sad consequence for a lifetime of poor choices was that he was trampled to death among the Zoramites while going from house to house begging for his food.

Heaven feels increasingly distant when we refuse to pay the price for gaining knowledge and peace. The Prophet Joseph taught, "The things of God are of deep import; and time, and experience, and careful and ponderous and solemn thoughts can only find them out."[10] In contrast, Satan offers instant gratification, usually requiring little to no effort on our part. His quick answers and

*Heaven feels increasingly distant when we refuse to pay the price for gaining knowledge and peace.*

temptations never build anything lasting or meaningful. God always helps us progress past ambiguity or temptation as we earnestly seek His truth and righteousness through His appointed sources.

## Forward with Faith

When ambiguity arises, we often ask, "Why doesn't the Lord just make things clearer and give more direct answers to our questions?" He seems content to follow His pattern of allowing uncertainty to linger as a defining part of our earthly test. This keeps us relying on Him as we seek for better ways to understand and faithfully move forward in the face of uncertainty.

Elder Richard G. Scott taught that Heavenly Father often gives "gentle promptings that require us to think, exercise faith, work, at times struggle, then act."[11] This is intended to be a process, not an event. Elder Scott continued, "His answers will seldom come while you are on your knees." He finished this thought by reminding us to be "thankful that sometimes God lets [us] struggle for a long time before that answer comes" because that allows us to move forward with faith and do the best we can with what we have already received.

CHAPTER 6

# Spirit Is Willing; Flesh Is Weak

*"O wretched man that I am! Yea, my heart sorroweth because of my flesh; my soul grieveth because of mine iniquities. . . . Nevertheless, I know in whom I have trusted."*
*—2 Nephi 4:17, 19*

During His mortal ministry, Jesus was invited to dine at the house of Simon, a Pharisee (see Luke 7:36). While there, a woman known as a sinner entered the house with an alabaster box of ointment. She then began washing Jesus' feet with her tears, wiping them with her hair, and anointing His feet with her balm (see v. 37–38). The Pharisee was surprised that Jesus would allow such a vile person to touch Him. Jesus responded with a short parable about a creditor with two debtors, one who owed a small amount and another who owed much. Both were forgiven. Jesus asked Simon which debtor would love the creditor most. Simon answered that the debtor forgiven the greatest amount would.

This scenario is one of many in the New Testament in which Jesus intercedes when a person is being judged or condemned by another. Whenever this occurred, Jesus never responded with a statement like, "Thank you for helping me recognize that she is a sinful woman." Instead, He always responded by redirecting the judgment back to the accuser(s). In this case, everyone, including the woman, was well aware of her spiritual struggles. Judgmental condemnation from the Pharisee, one who was supposed to be a shepherd in Israel, did not help improve her condition, but serving the Good Shepherd changed her life.

Jesus looked at the woman and said to Simon, "Seest thou this woman? I entered into thine house, thou gavest me no water for my feet: but she hath washed my feet with tears, and wiped them with the hairs of her head. Thou gavest me no kiss: but this woman since the time I came in hath not ceased to kiss my feet. My head with oil thou didst not anoint: but this woman hath anointed my feet with ointment" (Luke 7: 44–46). Jesus took the attention away from the woman's struggles and invited Simon to focus on himself rather than condemning her. The most touching part of the experience came when Jesus said, "Her sins, which are many, are forgiven; for she loved much. . . . And he said to the woman, Thy faith hath saved thee; go in peace" (v. 47, 50).

Robert Millet once shared what have become two of my favorite definitions: *Mercy:* To not get what we deserve, and *Grace:* To get what we don't deserve.[1] We have no scriptural reference where Jesus used the word *grace* in association with salvation, but His whole life embodied the principle. Everything He did and said was an extension of His grace. As for the woman stained with sin, His mercy shielded her from receiving what she deserved–judgment and condemnation. His grace, fueled by her faith, replaced the logical consequences with what she did *not* deserve–being cleansed and made whole.

Mercy: *To not get what we deserve.*

Grace: *To get what we don't deserve.*

Jesus knows better than any of us that our spirits are often willing but our flesh is weak (see Matthew 26:41). Thankfully, "God sent not his Son into the world to condemn the world" (John 3:17). One of the ultimate tests of discipleship is to internalize this doctrine by spending less time condemning ourselves or others for the opposition we all have within us and investing more time seeking to be transformed by Jesus' mercy and grace; He never turns truly repentant sinners away.

As we practice these principles, we find breaks in life's dark clouds and come to understand that we are surrounded by heavenly hosts that far outnumber the negative forces that seek to destroy us. We then find ways to build upon past successes to facilitate future triumphs, allow the Lord to be the one to identify our true weaknesses, work with Him to quickly recognize and fix our mistakes, become truer to the tests placed before us, and submit to the Savior as He cleanses us from sin that we cannot remove on our own.

## A Break in the Clouds

The Savior's mercy and grace extend to all of life's struggles, not just sin. Some time ago, my dear wife, Kiplin, wrestled with a difficult issue that deeply troubled her. We talked on many occasions but were unable to find answers. On one especially difficult day, we again sat down and discussed how Kiplin might find a measure of peace through the trial. As we talked, I finally realized and admitted that there was absolutely *nothing* I could say or do to lighten the burden. Both of us had willing spirits, but our flesh was truly weak. We had exhausted all of our own resources and keenly felt the reality of the statement: "And since man had fallen he could not merit anything of himself" (Alma 22:14).

That night, the Lord extended mercy and offered his grace. Kiplin recorded the experience as follows:

"Tyler and I settled in the front room and ended up having quite a long conversation. As we spoke, there were several moments where a light went on in my head *and* in my heart. I felt the quiet stirrings of answers forming. I felt some of the burden and weight of these struggles lift a little. I was able to feel light, *real* light, shining in 'the quiet heart' where are hidden 'sorrows that the eye can't see.' Sometimes it's hard to see the hand of the Lord in our struggles. We've been taught all our lives to walk in the light. I've decided that this is often a daily choice we have to make. Do we choose to turn to faith, hope, love, and joy, or do we choose doubt, anger, and fear?"

Kiplin held on with faith through many stormy months. Through that choice, she felt the Lord's grace carrying her through the deep waters, and eventually she experienced a break in the clouds.

## Opposition *IN* All Things

One major reason for our spiritual wrestles was taught by father Lehi to his young son Jacob: "For it must needs be, that there is an opposition in all things" (2 Nephi 2:11). We might prefer it if Lehi had said, "There is an opposition *to* all things." That way, we could blame most of our problems on external forces rather than acknowledging that the toughest battles we wage are usually internal. External opposition exists, but it serves to heighten the internal clash between our spirits and stubborn willfulness and pride—a true test of agency. According to Lehi, without opposition, "Righteousness could not be brought to pass, neither wickedness, neither holiness nor misery, neither good nor bad. Wherefore, all things must needs be a compound in one" (v. 11).

In mortality, we have opposing propensities and capacities for both good and evil. Too often, we allow our baser tendencies to win out, which leads to greater frustration and isolation from heaven. Yielding to our unrighteous inclinations increases the temptation to define ourselves by our sinfulness and failures rather than by our successes and desires for righteousness. When this happens, we allow our past self to hold our present self hostage. We win a major victory in this battle when we refuse to define ourselves by any past stage of our life. Turning to the Lord invites Him to break any bands of captivity we may be using to condemn ourselves.

*Turning to the Lord invites Him to break any bands of captivity we may be using to condemn ourselves.*

In William Shakespeare's play *As You Like It,* Duke Frederick was drastically changed by the charitable acts of his younger brother. Some who knew about his past had a hard time believing he had really changed. When asked if it was he who had actually tried to kill his younger brother at one time, he replied, "'Twas I; but 'tis not I: I do not shame to tell you what I was, since my conversion so sweetly tastes, being the thing I am."[2] We all need this newness of character, even though our change may not be as dramatic as Duke Frederick's.

## Transformation

I have long found inspiration from a story told by Ronald Frandsen, our bishop when we lived in Brigham City. He told of a man (I will call him John) who was an assistant branch clerk in a small town many years ago. At that time, things were handled a little differently than they are today. Each Sunday evening, John would balance the branch books in his living room with an ashtray on one corner of his desk and a cup of coffee or can of beer on the other. As time passed, the branch grew large enough to become a ward. The stake president called a new bishop and asked him to prayerfully pick his counselors. The bishop was inspired to call John as one of them. Though the stake president was initially shocked, he courageously extended the call.

He invited John into his office and informed him about the branch becoming a ward and told him who the new bishop would be.

Then he said, “John, the Lord has inspired this bishop to call you as one of his counselors.”

As Bishop Frandsen retold the story, John responded with something like, “President, you don’t understand; I smoke and I drink and I don’t pay my tithing.”

The inspired stake president replied back, “No, Brother John, *you* don’t understand. You *used* to smoke and you *used* to drink and you *used* to not pay your tithing.”

After a profound moment of silence and deep reflection, John agreed, “You’re right. I *don’t* smoke, and I *don’t* drink, and I *am* a full tithe payer. I will accept and fulfill the calling.” He immediately turned his life in a new direction and remained a diligent member of the Church until the day he died.

Bishop Frandsen noted, “Although there are some who say people change seldomly and slowly, I earnestly believe that there are scores of [people] in every stake who need us to show our confidence in them by asking them to do difficult things. They just need someone to take a chance on them. And why not? The Lord has taken a chance on each of us at various times in our lives.”[3]

Change doesn’t always have to be a long and drawn out process before we see fruits. In Bishop Frandsen’s own words, “Our past, be it good or less than admirable, means nothing. It is all in the rearview mirror, and we can’t do anything to change it. What matters is where we are headed right now. And we can all change directions in a split second.”[4] John was probably tempted on many subsequent occasions to drink and smoke again or to withhold his tithing. But he chose to stay on the new course offered him by the Lord and rely on the Lord’s help as he completed that course.

*Change doesn’t always have to be a long and drawn out process before we see fruits.*

President Henry B. Eyring spoke about the need for urgency in working on positive changes. He warned against the idea that we can just "go with the flow" and then repent later: "The flow has become a flood and soon will be a torrent. It will become a torrent of sounds and sights and sensations that invite temptation and offend the Spirit of God. Swimming back upstream to purity against the tides of the world was never easy. It is getting harder and may soon be frighteningly difficult."[5] We have more control over our lives than the devil would like us to believe. The sooner we make that commitment to change and seek God's grace in the process, the better.

## "They That Be With Us"

In the Old Testament, Syria waged war with Israel, but they were thwarted in their efforts because Elisha kept telling the King of Israel everything the Syrians were planning. Once the Syrian king learned of this, he became determined to capture Elisha—a bold decision considering that the prophet knew everything the king was plotting. The king's men found out that Elisha was in the village of Dothan. "Therefore sent he thither horses, and chariots, and a great host: and they came by night, and compassed the city about" (2 Kings 6:14).

The next morning, Elisha's servant rose early and saw the entire city surrounded by the Syrian host. How overwhelming that sight must have been for the servant! Elisha, on the other hand, was not intimidated by the Syrian army, because he had spiritual eyes to see what others could not. He calmed his servant's terrified cries by saying, "Fear not: for they that be with us are more than they that be with them" (2 Kings 6:16). You can imagine the lad's confusion. All he could see was the overwhelming might of the Syrian army. Elisha prayed and asked the Lord to open the eyes of the servant. "And the Lord opened the eyes of the young man; and he saw: and, behold, the mountain was full of horses and chariots of fire round about Elisha" (v. 17).

While this experience includes some humor, the reality for the servant was one of imminent doom. The prophetic vision and confidence emanating from Elisha, however, provided the needed perspective for the boy to hold on in faith. This is not vastly different from today. The secular tide is mounting all around us, appearing so vast in scope and so unstoppable in its advance that we feel there is nothing that can be done to hold it back. But in the work of the Lord, there will always be hope and deliverance for those who have eyes to see the angels sent to help us.

*In the work of the Lord, there will always be hope and deliverance for those who have eyes to see the angels sent to help us.*

Referring to his experience in Church councils, President Boyd K. Packer remarked, "I have seen, at times, great disappointment, some concern, maybe at times some anxiety. One thing I have never seen is fear. Fear is the antithesis of faith. In this Church and in this kingdom, there is faith."[6] We and our children will never be outnumbered as long as we are on the Lord's side. Countless angels from the unseen world will be there to buoy us up and defend us against the ominous powers of darkness.

## Future Triumphs

Captain Moroni is another wonderful example of how to respond when the oppositions of mortality seem too overpowering to fight on. Captain Moroni was initially able to overpower the more numerous Lamanite forces because he employed innovative defensive strategies (see Alma 43–50). At first, he gave his men the advantage of thick clothing and armor to defeat the much larger army of Zerahemnah.

The Lamanites learned from their mistake and outfitted their men with similar protections the next time they showed up for war. Unfortunately for them, Moroni did not rely on past successes to assure future victories.

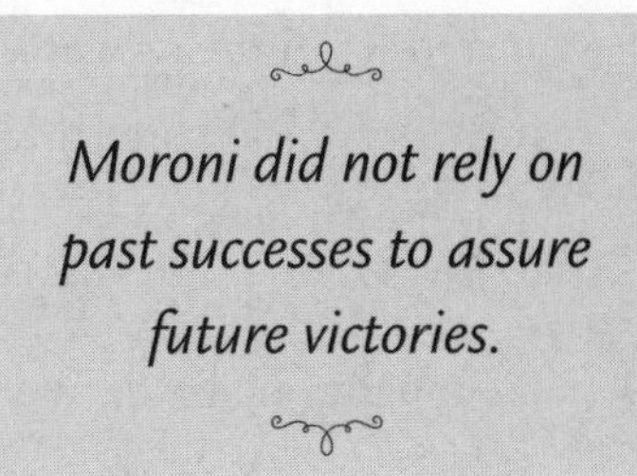


While the Lamanites were busy preparing for war with personal armor to be as protected as the Nephites, Moroni was casting up defensive banks of dirt around his cities. In such a setting, the Lamanite preparations were wasted, and they were slaughtered in the most one-sided defeat in the history of the Book of Mormon. Over a thousand Lamanites were killed, while not a single Nephite perished (see Alma 49:23). Moroni did not stop there. He knew the aggressions would continue. He fortified the banks of dirt with breastworks of timbers and towers to give his men even more advantage. He also fortified the border against future attacks.

This pattern of Moroni staying one step in front of the Lamanites forms an applicable pattern for us in our struggles against the powers of darkness. We cannot become complacent and assume that Satan won't adapt temptations and keep attacking our vulnerabilities. The best time to prepare defenses for future fights is right after we finish the current battle. Moroni's success would have likely continued if it hadn't been for the emergence of a much more dangerous enemy—the adversary within.

The kingmen rose up against their government, forcing Captain Moroni to call most of his soldiers away from their defensive strongholds to fight an internal war. The Lamanites took advantage of the Nephites' weakened condition and captured many of Moroni's fortified cities (see Alma 51:26 and 56:14). What had previously been a strength for the Nephites was now threatening to be their downfall.[7] It would have been easy for Moroni to become discouraged and surrender in the face of so much defeat. But he chose to fight on, giving us an ideal pattern for what to do when we lose spiritual ground in our own lives.

Moroni did not try to regain all of the captured cities at once. He fought one battle at a time until they were all reclaimed (see Alma 51–63). He knew this would be a long war, but he didn't allow the enormity of the task to overwhelm his daily efforts. If we, like Moroni, choose to keep the faith, trust the Lord, and focus on one battle at a time, we will eventually come off conquerors. As Elder Neal A. Maxwell put it, "What we insistently desire, over time, is what we will eventually become and what we will receive in eternity."[8]

When those battles drag out over decades or seem impossible to win, we can remember an important concept described by C. S. Lewis: "No man knows how bad he is till he has tried very hard to be good."[9] He went on to explain that some people believe that only those who sin really understand temptation. "This is an obvious lie. Only those who try to resist temptation know how strong it is." He described the strength of an army being discovered only when we fight it, not surrender to it. For this reason, it is not bad people who understand badness, but those who truly seek to be good. "We never find out the strength of the evil impulse inside us until we fight it." Lewis concluded this concept with Jesus as the ultimate example: "Christ, because He was the only man who never yielded to temptation, is also the only man who knows to the full what temptation means—the only complete realist." Our strength to resist temptations must come from the only One strong enough to overcome all of them.

*Our strength to resist temptations must come from the only One strong enough to overcome all of them.*

## Real Weakness

There is often a significant difference between our *true* and our *perceived* weakness. Near the end of the Book of Mormon, Moroni began translating and abridging the writings of the Jaredites. It appears he became more and more discouraged as he worked through this process. He was so powerfully moved by the written words on the Jaredite plates that he became increasingly self-conscious of his own limitations in writing. The brother of Jared had a few distinct advantages in this area. For one, he had experienced a remarkable vision, revealing to him all things from the beginning of time to the end of the world. Secondly, the brother of Jared wrote in a purer language that had not been confounded at the Tower of Babel. Imagine Moroni's frustration as he compared Jaredite capacity for expressive writing with his own abilities. The Nephites spoke an altered form of Hebrew, which had to be written in reformed Egyptian characters (see Mormon 9:32–33).

At one point, Moroni shifted focus away from his abridgment and began lamenting this struggle. "Lord, the Gentiles will mock at these things, because of our weakness in writing; for Lord thou hast made us mighty in word by faith, but thou hast not made us mighty in writing" (Ether 12:23). He went on to mention how awkward his hands were in the physical writing process.

> *There is power in letting the Lord, not the mirror, be the one to identify our weakness.*

A thoughtful analysis of Moroni's writing ability compared with other Book of Mormon authors does not prove him to be inferior. Why is it, then, that he felt so self-conscious? The Lord's response revealed that Moroni had likely misdiagnosed his real struggle: "And if men come unto me I will show unto them their weakness" (v. 27). There is power in letting the Lord, not the mirror, be the one to identify our weakness. He continued, "I give unto men weakness that they may be humble; and my grace is sufficient for all men that humble themselves before me; for if they humble themselves before me, and have faith in me, then will I make weak things become strong unto them." Notice that it is the Lord, not us, who makes us strong.

This passage never uses the word *weaknesses* (in the plural form); it only refers to God giving us *weakness*. There is a difference between *weakness* given by God and the *weaknesses* we bring upon ourselves through our choices. The Lord did not say, "I give unto men every struggle and imperfection they will ever face, to remind them to be humble." We are personally responsible for many of our limitations. But regardless of the source or cause of our weakness, He promises to "make weak things become strong."

In Moroni's case, he seems to have self-diagnosed his imperfection as, "I am a poor writer." If etching characters onto metal plates were Moroni's real weakness, then there should have been a marked improvement in his words after Ether 12:27. The writing in his latter chapters, however, doesn't appear to be different than that in his earlier chapters. The Lord possibly identified a more fundamental weakness than Moroni's writing difficulties—debilitating comparison that diminished his confidence. After that verse, Moroni only mentioned his weakness in writing one more time (see 12:40), but never again did he compare himself to the Jaredites. His own words show us how the Lord took a humble and faith-filled servant and helped him turn weakness into strength.

*The Lord will not judge us by placing us between the brother of Jared and Captain Moroni to see how well we measure up.*

This concept is helpful for us when we are tempted to compare our perceived weaknesses with the strengths of those around us. The Lord will not judge us by placing us between the brother of Jared and Captain Moroni to see how well we measure up. It is not helpful to compare our gifts, abilities, and callings to those of others. Heaven will feel nearer if we focus on what the Lord has given *us* and asked *us* to do rather than lamenting what we don't have or how well others are doing with what *they* have been given.

An extension of our need to identify our true weakness is helpful whenever we are tempted to berate ourselves while struggling with perfectionism. My friend Phillip Enkey shared the following insights with me: "For a long time I felt that Heavenly Father was expecting too much from me. How could I possibly meet all the standards required for exaltation? How could I possibly keep all of His commandments? It wasn't hard to feel constant doubt in the back of my mind that I would be able to keep any of this up for very long."[10] Phillip recognized that his desires were pure but his capacity to follow through on them would quickly fall short of perfection and create a feeling of distance from God through a perception of unworthiness. He continued, "Thanks to the insights shared by . . . others, I discovered for myself the power of the grace of Jesus Christ available through His Atonement. I began to believe Him when He said, 'As often as my people repent will I forgive them their trespasses against me' (Mosiah 26:30), and 'If ye will come unto me ye shall have eternal life. Behold, mine arm of mercy is extended towards you, and whosoever will come, him will I receive' (3 Nephi 9:14)."

Phillip's journey of discovery helped him understand that our judgment experience will not only include our works, as imperfect and inadequate as they may be, but the desires of our hearts as well. This reality caused him to wonder, *What is the adversary's angle? Doesn't he know that even when I struggle with sin, I can repent and be completely forgiven? Knowing that, why does he keep trying to get me to sin?* Phillip explained, "I believe the adversary uses the Lord's divine characteristic of perfect love against our own sense of fairness. He knows that our sins are no match for the Savior's grace." That means Satan's best chance is to get us to believe that we are not "save-able." He wants us to say, "It wouldn't be right or fair for Jesus to love me or forgive me after all that I have done wrong. I am not celestial material." Repetitious disobedience, if left without repentance, has the potential to incrementally shift our focus away from the Savior and adjust our desires toward lesser goals and telestial or terrestrial pursuits.

Phillip concluded, "Lucifer's goal is not to get us to commit sin so that we are disqualified from entering the celestial kingdom. Rather, he is tempting us so we convince ourselves that we are not worthy enough to go there. He wants us to sin enough times that we begin to believe we belong somewhere else."

## Mormon's Pattern

Moroni recognized that there could be imperfections in the record. On the Title Page of the Book of Mormon, he gave this disclaimer: "If there are faults they are the mistakes of men; wherefore, condemn not the things of God." In a variety of places, his father Mormon made little scribal errors on the plates. I point these out not to find fault with Mormon but to demonstrate how masterfully he responded to his mistakes.

In Alma 24, Mormon wrote, "And thus we see that they buried their weapons of peace" (v. 19). He recognized his initial mistake but couldn't hit delete or erase the faulty inscription on the metal plate, so he fixed the error with words, continuing, "or they buried the weapons of war, for peace" (v. 19). In another place, he told us that the Nephites were "shielded from the more vital parts of the body" (Alma 43:38). Taken literally, this would mean that they were guarded from dangerous body parts being thrown around the battlefield. Mormon's correction was, "or the more vital parts of the body being shielded from the strokes of the Lamanites."

The pattern is clear—Mormon recognized when he had made a mistake, he quickly corrected it, and then he moved on. I am grateful that the Lord allowed Mormon's minor slip-ups to come through in the translation process. They actually teach us a beautiful lesson about how we can approach our own missteps. Mormon demonstrated that we should not allow our mistakes to define us. We should recognize them, fix them, and move on.

*Mormon demonstrated that we should not allow our mistakes to define us. We should recognize them, fix them, and move on.*

## Covenants and Connections

A willingness to right our wrongs is a significant part of the baptismal covenant as described by Alma (see Mosiah 18). Alma's people desired to be called the people of God and come into His fold. To be God's people, they had to be willing "to bear one another's burdens, that they may be light; . . . to mourn with those that mourn; yea, and comfort those that stand in need of comfort" (v. 8–9). The next part of the covenant sets a seemingly impossible expectation: "To stand as witnesses of God at all times and in all things, and in all places that ye may be in, even until death" (v. 9). The word *all* sets the bar at perfection, with no wiggle room for minimizing the expectation!

Why would an all-knowing God ask imperfect, mortal children to make a promise that was impossible to keep? I believe the Lord sets the standard at perfection for a variety of reasons. One, we wouldn't perceive a need for Jesus Christ in order to just do our best. Knowing that man "could not merit anything of himself" (Alma 22:14) forces us to recognize our complete reliance on the Savior to have any hope of reaching His expectation. The Bible Dictionary teaches that it is "through the grace of the Lord that individuals . . . receive strength and assistance to do good works that they otherwise would not be able to maintain if left to their own means."[11]

Two, the whole point of a covenant is that we combine all our resources and efforts with the Savior's. His infinite perfection combined with our finite imperfection result in the covenant being kept "through the merits, and mercy, and grace of the Holy Messiah" (2 Nephi 2:8). A perfect, almighty, and all-knowing God actually seeks us out and asks us to bind ourselves to Him so He can help us become more like Him! *He* doesn't need this covenant to be saved, but we are eternally hopeless without it. King Benjamin made it clear that even if we were to serve God with all we have and all we are for the rest of our lives, we would still be "unprofitable servants"—meaning, God gives us more than we could ever give Him in return (see Mosiah 2:20–21).

What exactly does the covenantal language "stand as a witness of God" mean in practical terms? A witness is one who has personal knowledge of something and can testify of that truth. Witnesses are needed in a trial. Our secular world is accusing God of many things, such as not existing, being aloof, not being powerful enough to take away the world's evil and pain, and not knowing how to govern a complex world, to name just a few. Part of our covenant with Him is a willingness to stand as His witness against all these misunderstandings and accusations. He promises to "pour out his Spirit more abundantly" upon those who do so (Mosiah 18:10).

## True/False Tests

Truth seekers face many questions. *Is the Church true? Is the Book of Mormon true? Was Joseph a true prophet? Are we being led by true prophets today?* The world continues to probe deeper into these issues, searching for shreds of evidence that could discredit all claims of truth. As "the accuser of our brethren" (Revelation 12:10), the devil wants us to become skeptics of truth. The gospel, on the other hand, constantly invites us to ask, "Am *I* being true to the truths I know?"

Public opinion has no effect on eternal truth. All the belief or unbelief in the world cannot change "things as they really are" (Jacob

4:13). Even if everyone agreed that neither God nor gravity exists, that unanimous vote would not change the reality of either one—it would only change our perception and discourse regarding them. This is verified by the fact that only a tiny percentage of the world's population agreed with Jesus when He was preaching the greatest truths of eternity in Galilee and Judea. Time spent in the prosecuting attorney's seat, accusing God with various charges, is time we could have spent defending Him on the witness stand. In that role, we are most likely to discover truth and receive His help to pass our internal true/false tests.

## Steps toward Perfection

Often, the temptation in the process of becoming more perfect is to "run faster than [we have] strength" (Mosiah 4:27). God doesn't expect us to sprint up the pathway of discipleship and receive all promised blessings at once. He expects us to keep putting one foot in front of the other and to get back up when we fall down. Discipleship is a process, not an event. President James E. Faust encouraged steady progression rather than bursts of effort when he taught, "You cannot do everything well at the same time. You cannot be a 100 percent wife, a 100 percent mother, a 100 percent church worker, a 100 percent career person, and a 100 percent public-service person at the same time."[12] He encouraged a sequential approach to life, focusing on what is most essential at each stage. He said we "need not try to sing all of the verses" of our song at once.

*God doesn't expect us to sprint up the pathway of discipleship and receive all promised blessings at once. He expects us to keep putting one foot in front of the other and to get back up when we fall down. Discipleship is a process, not an event.*

Running faster than we have strength is one side of a pendulum swing. The opposite is falling into the trap of complacency, crying, "All is well in Zion!" (2 Nephi 28:21), thus stunting our growth. Worse yet, we might be tempted to take on an attitude of "prepentance"—saying, I can sin now and repent later with no lasting consequences: "Eat, drink, and be merry, for tomorrow we die; and it shall be well with us" (2 Nephi 28:7).

## Dragon Skin

Upward progression and positive change were never intended to be accomplished alone or in isolation from the Savior's redeeming grace. This principle is symbolically taught through C. S. Lewis' fictional character Eustace Scrubb in The Chronicles of Narnia, *Voyage of the Dawn Treader.* Through his own deliberate acts of selfishness, greed, and spite, Eustace was transformed into a loathsome dragon. His dragon form matched how the other characters felt about him. Eustace quickly grew weary of his new identity and wished above all else that he could somehow return to his human form and make things right with his companions, but there seemed to be no hope for that.

One night, Aslan, the Christ-figure lion, came into Eustace's valley and bade him follow. They stopped at a beautiful pool, high up in the mountains. Eustace desperately wanted to take a bath, but Aslan told him he would have to undress first. At that point, Eustace discovered that if he scratched his skin deep enough, the dragon scales would peel off like a snakeskin. With the scales cast aside, he approached the pool only to notice that he was still a dragon. Confused, he scratched another layer off, with the same outcome. He repeated this process multiple times with no improvement to his condition.

Aslan finally spoke to him: "You will have to let me undress you."[13] With no other hope, Eustace submissively laid back on the ground and let the lion do the tearing.

In the story, Eustace recounted: "The very first tear he made was so deep that I thought it had gone right into my heart. And when he began pulling the skin off, it hurt worse than anything I've ever felt. The only thing that made me able to bear it was just the pleasure of feeling the stuff peel off."[14] Aslan did what no one else could, and Eustace was given a new chance at life.

Although this is a fictional story, it teaches the beautiful reality that we must allow Jesus to do the deep, life-changing operations on our soul. We are powerless to save ourselves; *Jesus* is our appointed Savior and Redeemer. God never intended for us to save ourselves or overcome evil in isolation. Our job is to turn our lives over to Him and submit to His dragon-skin removal process that frees us from past sins, addictions, and weakness, and allows us to truly have a newness of life.

> *God never intended for us to save ourselves or overcome evil in isolation.*

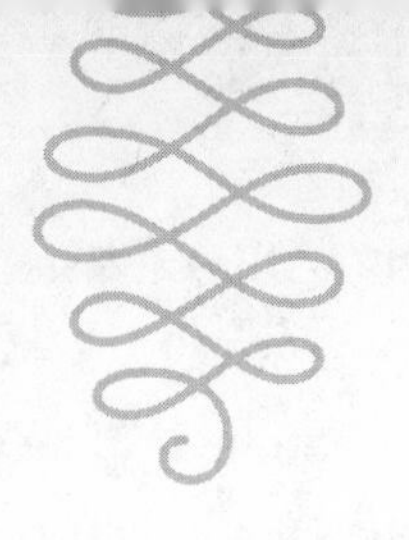

CHAPTER 7

# When Loved Ones Struggle

*"I am poured out like water, and all my bones are out of joint: my heart is like wax; it is melted."*
*—Psalm 22:14*

Few things are more painful than seeing loved ones make unwise choices. After all, we can't live the gospel for them. We can't force inspiration upon them or vicariously build their testimonies. It can leave us feeling like the helpless characters in the old poem "Humpty Dumpty." There was nothing anyone could do to "fix" his problems. When dealing with loved ones who struggle, I prefer a more hopeful version of this poem, shared by Elder Vaughn J. Featherstone: "Humpty Dumpty sat on a wall, Humpty Dumpty had a great fall; All the king's horses and all the king's men couldn't put Humpty Dumpty together again. But the *king* could, and the king *can*, and the king *will* if we will but come unto him."[1]

An eternal perspective is essential for understanding possible reasons why there are so many Humpty Dumpty-like falls in our world today. We are surrounded by a prophesied crescendo of violence, corruption, and immorality on the same planet that crucified the Creator of worlds without end. Many stumble and withdraw from the warm light of heaven and find themselves trapped in bondage, pain, and despair. The Lord assures us that He loved our loved ones long before

He brought them into our lives, and He will help us work with them, even if they have lost all hope.

## This Planet We Call Home

Our earth is a very unique place. Understanding this gives us greater tolerance and capacity to help those who choose to wander on "strange roads" or "forbidden paths" (1 Nephi 8:28, 32). During his ministry, Enoch was caught up into heaven and shown a sweeping vision of the history of the earth (see Moses 7). He recorded an important sequence of events that reveals significant insights regarding this particular planet: "And he beheld Satan; and he had a great chain in his hand, and it veiled the whole face of the earth with darkness; and he looked up and laughed, and his angels rejoiced" (v. 26). Notice that "the whole face of the earth" was veiled by the devil's power. It's hard to imagine what it must have been like for Enoch to see Satan looking up at God and laughing as the devils rejoiced over the spread of wickedness and suffering. I picture Enoch feeling a great desire to return to the earth to push back that evil chain and stop the devils' rejoicing.

The next verse speaks of angels descending from heaven, bearing testimony of the Father and the Son. At that point in the vision, Enoch saw God weeping over the "residue of the people" (v. 28). This confused him, and he asked the Lord how He could weep, considering the fact that "were it possible that man could number the particles of the earth, yea, millions of earths like this, it would not be a beginning to the number of thy creations" (v. 30). Enoch couldn't understand why the Lord would weep

> *"I can stretch forth mine hands and hold all the creations which I have made; and mine eye can pierce them also, and among all the workmanship of mine hands there has not been so great wickedness as among thy brethren."*

over the suffering He saw on one little planet when He had innumerable creations. As part of His answer, God made a stunning declaration: "I can stretch forth mine hands and hold all the creations which I have made; and mine eye can pierce them also, and among all the workmanship of mine hands there has not been so great wickedness as among thy brethren" (v. 36). If interpreted literally, the Lord told Enoch that among worlds without number (see Moses 1:32–33), there is greater wickedness on this earth than anywhere else in the vast expanse of His universe.

We learn in Moses 1:32–33, 37 that God's Only Begotten Son is the Creator of those numberless worlds. Once again, if these scriptures are interpreted literally, that means Jesus Christ has created more worlds than can be comprehended. Regarding the scope and scale of Jesus' place in our Heavenly Father's plan, D&C 76:24 tells us, "That by him, and through him, and of him, the *worlds* are and were created, and the inhabitants thereof are begotten sons and daughters unto God" (emphasis added). Joseph Smith created a poetic retelling of section 76 for W. W. Phelps:

*And I heard a great voice bearing record from heav'n,*
*He's the Saviour and only begotten of God;*
*By him, of him, and through him, the worlds were all made,*
*Even all that career in the heavens so broad.*

*Whose inhabitants, too, from the first to the last,*
*Are sav'd by the very same Saviour of ours;*
*And, of course, are begotten God's daughters and sons*
*By the very same truths and the very same powers.*[2]

Living on the same planet as the Creator and Savior of worlds without number causes us to pause and consider our own place in God's vast plan. Of all the places in the universe we might have been sent, why did we end up here, on the same planet where Jesus lived

His mortal life, surrounded by such great wickedness? The difficulty of our circumstance is magnified because we live in the dispensation of the fullness of times. Based on the Savior's parable of the wheat and tares, this "fullness" does not refer exclusively to the growing kingdom of God on the earth; the kingdom of the devil is also increasing in every way like never before.

There was never a time with greater righteousness across the world. There are more temples, more missions, more people using priesthood power, more family history resources, more teaching tools, more scripture study tools, and more miracles spreading into all corners of the earth than ever before. Conversely, there is also more wickedness. People worldwide have greater access to evil than in any other period of the earth's history, and multitudes are embracing it. President Gordon B. Hinckley summarized this polarity: "Notwithstanding the great evil of these times, what a glorious season it has been and now is. A new day has come in the work of the Almighty. That work has grown and strengthened and moved across the earth. It has now touched for good the lives of millions, and this is only the beginning."[3]

*Understanding the "degree of difficulty" associated with* this *particular earth, in* this *dispensation, should help us employ more godly tolerance for those who struggle—especially ourselves.*

Without ignoring the growing wickedness that surrounds us, we have a unique opportunity to focus our efforts on the amazing blessing it is to live at a time when our potential for good has never been greater. Understanding the "degree of difficulty" associated with *this* particular earth, in *this* dispensation, should help us employ more godly tolerance for those who struggle—especially ourselves.

## *E Pluribus Unum*

Our need to come together and help each other, especially when someone feels weak, is symbolically taught in an unexpected place—the back of a US $1 bill (in the right-hand circle of the Seal of the United States). This circle depicts an eagle holding an olive branch and arrows. This drawing uses thirteen leaves, berries, arrows, stripes, and stars to depict the thirteen original colonies, which also became the first states to unite. The eagle's banner, also with thirteen letters, declares the foundational principle for the newly formed nation: *E Pluribus Unum.* This Latin phrase means, "from many, one" or "out of many, one." Thirteen separate and distinct states unified as one nation—the United States. These states joined the union without giving up their own unique identities and distinctiveness.

The individual states vowed to be one with the others in their times of peace (the olive branch), war (arrows), defense (shield), and when seeking truth and intelligence (stars). This same *E Pluribus Unum* principle is perfectly manifest in the Godhead. It also holds true for successful families or congregations.

Paul taught, "The body is one, and hath many members, and all the members of that one body, being many, are one body" (1 Corinthians 12:12). Paul then described the need for a wide variety of parts in a physical body. If every member of a family or congregation had the same abilities and gifts, they would also share the same weaknesses and inabilities. Because of our uniqueness, loved ones usually see things differently than we do or struggle with things we do not.

When we break a bone or injure a certain part of our body, we don't punish it for getting hurt. Quite the opposite—we treat it with great gentleness and increased care. After all, we know that broken bones and injuries usually heal when we take proper steps to provide a healing environment. The parts of our body that need the most attention and care are the ones that hurt the most or that are weakest. The same is true of individuals in our circle of influence. "The members should have the same care one for another. And whether one member suffer, all the members suffer with it; or one member be honoured, all the members rejoice with it" (1 Corinthians 12:25–26).

When people sin or get spiritually injured, they hurt, and a part of them longs to feel whole again. We don't encourage healing by heaping further insult or condemnation upon them. We can, however, extend support, empathy, and, if needed, appropriate boundaries and limitations to prevent further damage from occurring. The degree and length of the injury determines the amount of healing support that will be needed to facilitate recovery.

## Variations on Deliverance

The Book of Mosiah demonstrates two contrasting examples of deliverance and healing. Limhi and Alma's groups both escaped Lamanite bondage and returned to the safety of Zarahemla, but the underlying details in their experiences reveal major differences that teach us valuable lessons today. When helping loved ones work through spiritual bondage, the principles of deliverance in both of these experiences are helpful and inspiring.

Limhi's people were brought into bondage immediately after the death of his father, King Noah. At the outset, they were oppressed with a fifty-percent tax and sore burdens. They realized that "there was no way that they could deliver themselves out of their hands, for the Lamanites had surrounded them on every side" (Mosiah 21:5). In spite of that realization, they murmured until the king let them attack the Lamanites. Limhi's people somehow convinced themselves that they would win a battle even though they were surrounded and outnumbered in every way. Rather than improving their situation, all of their previous problems became much worse when they were defeated and many were killed.

Rather than turning to the Lord, they decided to fight the Lamanites again. The second battle went no better than the first. The burden of providing for the physical needs of the people in addition to the required tribute tax was being laid on fewer and fewer shoulders. The people went to battle a third time, with the same outcome as before. Abinadi had prophesied to these people that they would be brought into bondage for their refusal to repent. He also informed them that unless they repented while in bondage, they would be utterly destroyed from off the face of the earth (see Mosiah 12:8).

Limhi's group finally turned to the Lord after more than twenty years of struggling and fighting to deliver themselves from slavery. They were humbled "even in the depths of humility; and they did cry mightily to God; yea, even all the day long did they cry unto their God that he would deliver them out of their afflictions" (Mosiah 12:14). Only after they turned to Him did God rescue them by sending a group of men from Zarahemla to facilitate their escape.

In contrast to this story, Alma's righteous people spent those same twenty-plus years in peace and prosperity building up the city of Helam. Mormon introduced their brief bondage experience by saying, "The Lord seeth fit to chasten his people; yea, he trieth their patience and their faith. Nevertheless—whosoever putteth his trust in him the same shall be lifted up at the last day" (Mosiah 23:21–22). The Lamanite army that got lost in the wilderness while chasing Limhi's group stumbled across Alma's people, who didn't wait years to turn to the Lord. Even before the Lamanite army made it to their city, they had turned to their prophet for guidance. Alma calmed their fears and reminded them that "they should remember the Lord their God and he would deliver them. Therefore they hushed their fears, and began to cry unto the Lord that he would soften the hearts of the Lamanites, that they would spare them, and their wives, and their children" (v. 27–28).

Amulon was given control over Alma's people, and he made their bondage as miserable as he could. He put taskmasters over them and commanded them to stop praying. They continued pleading in their hearts, and the Lord responded, "Lift up your heads and be of good comfort, for I know of the covenant which ye have made unto me; and I will covenant with my people and deliver them out of bondage" (Mosiah 24:13). God also promised to "ease the burdens which are put upon your shoulders, that even you cannot feel them upon your backs, even while you are in bondage; and this will I do that ye may stand as witnesses for me hereafter, and that ye may know of a surety that I, the Lord God, do visit my people in their afflictions" (v. 14). With that promise, "The burdens which were laid upon Alma and his brethren were made light; yea, the Lord did strengthen them that they could bear up their burdens with ease, and they did submit cheerfully and with patience to all the will of the Lord" (v. 15). Not long after this, the Lord miraculously delivered the people to safety.

*When we seek to deliver ourselves from serious sins or problems without the Lord's help, things usually get worse and the bondage becomes heavier and lasts longer.*

Even though both groups ended up in Zarahemla, Limhi's group arrived bruised, broken, and considerably diminished in numbers compared to Alma's people, who arrived fairly unscathed and even strengthened by their bondage experiences in the land of Nephi. When we seek to deliver ourselves from serious sins or problems without the Lord's help, things usually get worse and the bondage becomes heavier and lasts longer.

## Lost and Found

On one occasion, Jesus was eating with known sinners and publicans—two groups judged as unclean by the self-righteous Pharisees and

Scribes. They murmured against Jesus for spending time with such sinful people and called His character into question for eating with them. In response to their condemnation, Jesus told three related parables about things that got lost but were eventually found (see Luke 15).

In the first parable, a good shepherd left ninety-nine of his sheep to go and find one lost sheep. All through my growing-up years, this parable confused me. I wondered why a good shepherd would leave the flock and risk losing more sheep in an effort to rescue *one.* Joseph Smith shared prophetic commentary regarding this parable. He explained how he found meaning in the parables and other teachings of Jesus: "I have a key by which I understand the scripture—I enquire, what was the question which drew out the answer."[4] In this case, the self-righteous were questioning Jesus' association with sinners. Joseph went on to interpret this parable by saying that the angels rejoice over "one sinner that repenteth" more than over ninety-and-nine self-congratulatory persons who are "so righteous they will be damned anyhow; you cannot save them."[5] The Pharisees didn't feel lost and consequently felt no need for a spiritual shepherd. On the other hand, the sinners eating with Jesus knew they were lost and recognized their desperate need to be found.

Jesus' second parable was similar to the first in many ways. One coin in ten was lost. The coin didn't wander away as the sheep had; it was lost out of neglect. By no fault of its own, it was no longer in the pocket with the other coins. The woman of the house swept every corner of her house until she found it and came again rejoicing.

The final parable involved the loss of something much more valuable than a sheep or a coin. The story began with the younger of two sons asking for his inheritance while his father was still alive—a request that was both disrespectful and disgraceful. The father consented and the young man soon departed, carrying wealth he had not earned himself.

He traveled to a far country, where he began to squander his newly acquired fortune. Many wonder why the father did not go after his son to find him and bring him home, as the good shepherd had done with the lost sheep and the woman had done with the coin. The answer lies, perhaps, in the difference between how each of the three things became lost in the first place.

Sheep get lost because they have a propensity to put their heads down, start eating, and wander away. The coin got lost out of neglect. In both cases, the right thing to do was search for them until they were found. The prodigal son was different; he *chose* to rebel. He left of his own free will. If his father had gone into the far country to bring him home, the son would have likely withdrawn further, with increased bitterness and resentment. What can be done to help prodigals like this young man? The remaining details of the parable might help us with possible answers to that question.

As is usually the case with rebellion, the time came when "there arose a mighty famine in that land; and he began to be in want" (Luke 15:14). The only job the young man could get was feeding pigs. This part of Jesus' story would have gotten the Pharisees' attention! Swine were abhorred by Jews in the first century. To make matters worse, the lost son became so destitute and hungry that he wanted to eat the pigs' slop but was not allowed to (see v. 16). Then came the critical turning point: "And when *he came to himself,* he said . . . I will arise and go to my father, and will say unto him, Father, I have sinned against heaven, and before thee, and am no more worthy to be called thy son" (v. 17–19; emphasis added). Prodigals, or those who knowingly rebel, need to decide for *themselves* to return. This often happens when they hit rock bottom and "come to themselves." Loving efforts to cry repentance or teach them before that point may only serve to push them further away and delay the much-needed wake-up call.

The prodigal's return journey was poignant: "And he arose, and came to his father. But when he was yet a great way off, his father saw him, and had compassion" (Luke 15:20). The fact that his father saw him so far away implied that he had been watching the road, tirelessly waiting for the first sign of his lost son's return. Most parents would be furious at the boy for squandering their hard-earned money, but not this father; he ran *to* his child. He was not put off by his son's deplorable physical condition. Underneath all the pig stench, the sweat from a long journey, and the stain of countless poor decisions, was a son of God. His tattered rags and starving condition did not keep this father from taking his broken son in his arms and kissing him. He brought him home and clothed him in his best robe, gave him shoes and a ring, and killed the fatted calf. We may not be able to go into a far country and pull our loved ones out of their pig stalls, but we can patiently hope, believe, watch, fast, and pray for that day when they make the first effort to return home—and then we can run to them with open arms and forgiving hearts.

*Underneath all the pig stench, the sweat from a long journey, and the stain of countless poor decisions, was a son of God.*

Ironically, the only person in the story who is upset about the prodigal son's return is the older brother. Based on Joseph Smith's key for interpreting parables, we could all benefit from recognizing where we have demonstrated prodigal tendencies and meekly approach Heavenly Father and plead for His forgiveness. The pharisaical alternative is to tell God about how righteous we have been and how we have never rebelled nor squandered any inheritance, like the older son did in the parable.

Considering the three parables, a key for parents and others who have loved ones that are lost is to better understand how that has happened. Did they *wander* away from the fold unwittingly? Did family members, teachers, leaders, or others *neglect* them? Or did they knowingly and willingly *rebel* against the truth? Granted, life is complex, and the answer to this question might be a combination of reasons. But by seeking a better understanding of our loved ones' underlying motivations, we will have a better idea of how to help them. In the case of prodigals, many parents must patiently and prayerfully watch that road for years, decades, or even a lifetime. In some cases, that faithful vigilance stretches into the next life. Even though heaven may be far from the thoughts and desires of the rebellious child, it can be close for faithful parents amidst painful tears and sleepless nights.

*Even though heaven may be far from the thoughts and desires of the rebellious child, it can be close for faithful parents amidst painful tears and sleepless nights.*

Heavenly Parents are doing everything they can, short of taking away agency, to bring that child back to the safety of your arms. If prodigals feel their family's love and acceptance, even while knowing the family doesn't condone all of their choices, they are more likely to return home for help and direction when they finally "come to themselves."

Elder Jeffrey R. Holland spoke clearly about the kind of love and devotion we need to reach out through time and space into those dark places to urge lost ones to come home. He used words such as "Bear, borne, carry, [and] deliver" [6] to describe what the Savior does for all of us. Especially in the case of prodigals, Elder Holland explained, "These words also connote burden, struggle, and fatigue—words most appropriate in describing the mission of Him who, at unspeakable cost, lifts us up when we have fallen, carries us forward when strength is gone, delivers us safely home when safety seems far beyond our reach." Elder Holland taught that the one thing that most closely approximates these supernal efforts is "the selfless love of a devoted mother." Parents of prodigal children know that they cannot prevent their children from hurting themselves and others. But they *can* love them and hold on to hope.

## Stay at the Tree

What if family members or loved ones persist in negative behavior and refuse to respond to our love? Perhaps father Lehi and mother Sariah could give us wise counsel in those cases. Their two oldest sons had become so hardened that they tried to kill Nephi and plotted to kill their father as well. In his dream, Lehi saw them refuse to come and partake of the fruit. But Lehi and Sariah did not leave the tree because of their sons' refusal to join them.

When a loved one faces serious issues, some families feel torn between clinging to the gospel and reaching out to the struggling individual. This need not be a mutually exclusive choice. Nobody in Lehi's dream left the tree of life to help another person. Only by staying firm in the faith can we provide a foundation for strugglers to return and rebuild their own faith. We do not know all the reasons why each child is sent to his or her specific family, but all children will benefit from parents who love them without compromising God's laws and expectations.

*Only by staying firm in the faith can we provide a foundation for strugglers to return and rebuild their own faith.*

## When Consequences Linger

Sometimes, a prodigal child returns to loving arms but struggles with natural consequences far longer than we or they expect. I have spoken with individuals who openly lament how hard it is to battle addictions even after they return to the faith. On one occasion, an individual shouted in exasperation, "Why won't God just take this away from me? I believe! I'm trying! I know He can do this, so why doesn't He?" That is an important question. We can't talk ourselves out of something we have behaved ourselves into. It is rare to live through years of serious sin and then turn around in a few weeks or months.

God is not to blame when people make decisions that are unwise or that put them in harm's way. Natural consequences follow every choice, and some of those consequences might never be removed in this life. It is possible to be fully forgiven by the Lord and the Church and still deal with intense, lingering consequences that stretch over years.

We can facilitate recovery, but we cannot control it. This is similar to physical healing. We can't force the body to heal after an injury, but we can provide treatment, medicines, and therapies to *facilitate* recovery. Once we have taken those steps, we must patiently wait for the body to work through its natural healing process. The deeper the wound, the greater the need for patience and diligence in that healing. In the case of spiritual wounds, we can provide loving support and healing balm, but the actual healing and restoration process are the Savior's domain.

During prolonged recuperation, we may grow weary and yearn for the day that we can go to heaven and escape all this pain. We falsely assume that God will save us from this earth and take us away to heaven. The reality is that God is bringing heaven to us.[7] Taking part in that transition from earth to heaven requires purging and purifying; it will require deep and permanent change. For that reason, we must trust the Lord even when He doesn't take away consequences or struggles,

> *The Lord will not require anyone to suffer one moment longer than is absolutely necessary for his or her eternal benefit.*

because there must be more purging and refining needed. Those physical addictions and weaknesses will not be part of our resurrected bodies. The Lord will not require anyone to suffer one moment longer than is absolutely necessary for his or her eternal benefit.

## Old Wounds

Not all homecomings are filled with joy and rejoicing. Sometimes, a prodigal's return produces deep pain or opens tender wounds for those who were betrayed or hurt by past wrongs. In these situations, offended parties need the grace of the Savior just as the offender does. They need the power to forgive. They need the Lord to wash away resentment and replace the pain with sweet mercy and the ability to trust and love once again. Gratefully, Jesus' power is not limited to cleansing returning prodigals; He equally specializes in binding up broken hearts left in their wake.

When the Lamanites launched an attack on King Noah's people, the king fled before them into the wilderness (see Mosiah 19). As a symbolic type of the devil, Noah placed himself at the front of those fleeing, using his people as a shield for his own safety (see v. 9). This left the most vulnerable group of people at the back, undefended, where the Lamanites began to overtake and slay them. King Noah concluded that the women and children were slowing them down, so he commanded his men to save their own lives by leaving their families and following him further into the wilderness (see v. 11). Many of the men refused to obey this command, but the rest followed Noah, abandoning their families to the enemy. Imagine the shock and dismay of the wives and children as they watched those men running away, leaving them at the mercy of the Lamanites.

The devil's message to mankind today is exactly the same as it was on that day through the mouth of King Noah: "Leave your families and follow me out into this enticing wilderness where you can take care of *your* needs and *your* wants." Today's alluring wildernesses are vices such as immoral relationships, pornography, drugs, alcohol, video games, gambling, or excessive focus on money, work, entertainment, sports, or any number of self-centered and devilish pursuits.

Noah and his followers fled until they knew they were no longer being followed; they finally felt safe. But it didn't take long for these men to come to a horrible realization—they may have temporarily *saved* their lives, but they had lost everything of real value *in* their lives! Comprehending their terrible mistake, they determined to go back and give up their lives by fighting the Lamanites. After burning King Noah, they returned to the spot where they had forsaken their families and were told that their wives and children had not been killed but were now enslaved by the Lamanites. They returned to the city "rejoicing, because their wives and their children were not slain" (Mosiah 19:24).

This was glorious news for those men! The part of this experience that the Book of Mormon does not recount, however, was their actual homecoming. What was it like when these men first walked into their homes? What could they *possibly* say or do to make things right? This would have been one of the most difficult moments of life for all involved. We often emphasize what returning sinners feel when asking to be forgiven. But there is an equally painful process that sometimes gets overlooked; what is it like for the person who was betrayed?

Imagine the pain of the women and children as these men came home and asked to be pardoned. These families had been completely forsaken, utterly abandoned, and intentionally left to be destroyed. One does not simply brush this level of treachery aside without divine aid. These families, just like loved ones today, needed the Savior's mercy and grace to rebuild shattered trust.

## Trees and Men

Some people blame their poor decisions on others or on difficult circumstances caused by their upbringing. This victim mentality can lead to deeper sin, causing increased frustration and feeding the false belief that God does not care.

Lehi addressed this issue right before his death while blessing his son Jacob. He acknowledged that his young son had experienced an unusually difficult life up to that point: "Thou art my firstborn in the days of my tribulation in the wilderness. And behold, in thy childhood thou hast suffered afflictions and much sorrow, because of the rudeness of thy brethren" (2 Nephi 2:1). But rather than commiserating with him and dwelling on the injustices of his past, father Lehi focused Jacob on the Lord's goodness: "Nevertheless, Jacob, my firstborn in the wilderness, thou knowest the greatness of God; and he shall consecrate thine afflictions for thy gain" (v. 2). Jacob's difficult childhood provided opportunities for the Lord to manifest His merciful power in ways that forever blessed this future prophet and those he taught.

This principle is reiterated in Zenos' allegory of the olive trees (see Jacob 5). At one point, one of the servants questioned the lord's wisdom in planting a particular tree in what he judged to be the "poorest spot in all the land of thy vineyard" (v. 21). The lord of the vineyard began to teach this servant about soils and fruitfulness: "Counsel me not; I knew that it was a poor spot of ground" (v. 22). The Lord knows when and where to send each child for his or her greatest potential benefit. He is infinitely aware of every limitation when He plants a tree or a child in a "poor spot of ground."

The lord of the vineyard explained, "I have nourished it this long time, and thou beholdest that it hath brought forth much fruit." Knowing that the tree would get little nourishment from the poor soil, the lord nourished it himself. The servant was focused on the ground, but the lord stayed focused on the tree and its fruit.

To accentuate this point, the lord of the vineyard showed the servant a different tree planted in worse soil than the first (v. 23). That tree was also growing and producing much fruit thanks to the lord's watchful care and nourishment.

Finally, the lord of the vineyard took the servant to one of the best spots of ground in all the vineyard and showed him a tree planted there. "Only a part of the tree hath brought forth tame fruit, and the other part of the tree hath brought forth wild fruit; behold, I have nourished this tree like unto the others" (v. 25).

## Producing Fruit

The Lord is not limited by our past abuses, neglect, and scars. He is well aware of all our limitations, but He is also a master at growing, shaping, and helping trees become fruitful. He perfectly knows how and when to dig, nourish, prune, graft, or burn branches. When working through deep struggles with a loved one, we can benefit from recognizing the Master's efforts as we see each of these shaping influences being employed in their behalf.

*The Lord is not limited by our past abuses, neglect, and scars. He is well aware of all our limitations, but He is also a master at growing, shaping, and helping trees become fruitful.*

Digging around the roots is not a comfortable experience for a tree. Some of the smaller surface roots are bound to get severed, thus encouraging the tree to send its roots deeper into the soil. Breaking up the ground is also necessary to allow moisture and nutrients to better soak into the dirt where the tree can absorb them. People are a lot like trees in this way. Without humility, life-enhancing lessons are less likely to sink in and become part of us. It is not helpful to throw nutrient-rich fertilizer onto hard-packed earth or hardened hearts. Most of it will wash away.

Pruning is also an essential technique used by the Lord. If left without care, a fruit tree will grow out of control. It will seek to produce wood and leaves rather than fruit.[8] When a tree gets pruned appropriately, it transfers more energy into fruit production. For us, the Master Gardener occasionally comes into our lives with pruning shears and a saw. Relationships or pursuits that took years for us to grow can be cut off and taken out of our lives in a matter of moments. Pruning, though painful, can help us redirect and focus our energy to branches where the Lord wants us to produce more fruit.

*Pruning, though painful, can help us redirect and focus our energy to branches where the Lord wants us to produce more fruit.*

Grafting is a way for a husbandman to bring new opportunities for potential fruit to a tree. The Gardener of our souls knows which new relationships and opportunities we need in our life. He also knows the best timing for grafting in these new branches.

When loved ones are struggling, it is more difficult for them to recognize the blessings of the Lord's digging, pruning, and grafting efforts. This is where family members and leaders can help them understand potential reasons the Lord gives and takes away certain things. Jesus knows what He is doing with his trees *and* His disciples.

## Trust Jesus

Elder Jeffrey R. Holland told of his four-year old neighbor, Katie Lewis, who had an older brother suffering from leukemia. Katie's parents sought peace and healing through much fasting, prayer, and temple worship. One day, Sister Lewis returned home after an exhausting day and little Katie came running up to her, clutching a sheaf of papers. She extended these to her mother and asked, "Mommy, do you know what these are?"

Her mother's weary response was, "No, Katie. I don't know what they are. Please tell me."

"They are the scriptures, and do you know what they say?"

At this point, Elder Holland recounted, "Sister Lewis stopped smiling, gazed deeply at this little child, knelt down to her level, and said, 'Tell me, Katie. What do the scriptures say?'

"'They say, "Trust Jesus."' And then she was gone."

As Sister Lewis stood back up with that crumpled stack of papers covered with a four-year-old's writing, "She felt near-tangible arms of peace encircle her weary soul and a divine stillness calm her troubled heart." Elder Holland concluded by saying, "I too say, 'Trust Jesus.' Let him still the tempest and ride upon the storm. Believe that he can lift mankind from its bed of affliction, in time and in eternity." [9]

CHAPTER 8

# "Draw Near unto Me and I Will Draw Near unto You"

*"Nothing is going to startle us more when we pass through the veil to the other side than to realize how well we know our Father and how familiar His face is to us."*[1]
*—President Ezra Taft Benson*

When I ask my students how old they are, they naturally respond by giving me their ages in earth years. We instinctively define ourselves within the bookends of mortal birth and death, even though Joseph Smith clearly taught, "The intelligence of Spirits had no beginning neither will it have an end."[2] In the words of Eliza R. Snow, "Ofttimes a secret something whispered, 'You're a stranger here.' And I felt that I had wandered from a more exalted sphere."[3] Thinking outside the margins of mortality helps us focus on our true identity and future potential. It helps us recognize that heaven is nearer than our mortal perception can grasp.

*Thinking outside the margins of mortality helps us focus on our true identity and future potential. It helps us recognize that heaven is nearer than our mortal perception can grasp.*

No matter how small or insignificant our efforts may seem, as we strive to draw near to Heavenly Father through Jesus Christ, we will come to better understand Their perfection. The Holy Ghost will facilitate our efforts to connect with God through deep and meaningful prayer, and He will guide our understanding of the various answers we receive in response. He will also help us take our scripture study to new levels of historical and doctrinal understanding as we increasingly find our own story reflected on the pages. The Holy Spirit will help us find greater connection with God when we walk in sacred space where Jesus walks and when we do the right things for the right reasons, like going to church, fulfilling our callings, and fasting with perspective. Heaven will also draw nearer when we surround ourselves with inspiring music, media, and uplifting entertainment.

## Overemphasizing Jesus?

Years ago, I was asked to help develop an online seminary program. I submitted my lesson material for First Nephi and then met with representatives from Church Correlation for their feedback and training. They began by saying, "Tyler, you have overemphasized Christ in your lessons." I chuckled, thinking this was a joke. When I realized they were serious, I became confused. I wondered how it was possible to overemphasize Jesus in a book subtitled "Another Testament of Jesus Christ."

The leader of the group kindly explained to me that members of the Church have been accused for so long of not being Christian that we often overcorrect by emphasizing Jesus to the point of ignoring our Heavenly Father. In that moment, I knew exactly what he had meant about overemphasizing Christ. I had not included anything in my lessons about God the Father. Our *first* relationship was not with Jesus; it was with Heavenly Father. Jesus Christ Himself emphasized the Father when He taught in Third Nephi. This was a wakeup call for me. The committee didn't ask me to take anything out of my lessons that referred to the Savior; they just suggested that I include the Father in places where it was appropriate.

Without this correction, students may have been confused about Jesus' role in the Father's plan. Based on His own words and example in scripture, we learn that Jesus never intended for our progression to end by coming to Him. As our Mediator, Jesus desires to bring us to the Father and plead our case before Him (see D&C 45:3–5).

Another example of overemphasizing a principle comes in the form of overemphasizing the Atonement. President Russell M. Nelson spoke about this issue in his April 2017 general conference address. If we are not careful, we might say that *the Atonement* saves us from sin, addictions, temptations, and sorrow. We might be well intentioned, but phrases such as "rely on the Atonement for deliverance" or "turn to the Atonement" can take our focus off of Christ. Nowhere in scripture does it say, "Come unto the Atonement and be perfected in it." The Atonement is not something that exists independent of God and Jesus. It is not an entity unto itself, and it can do nothing for us in isolation. It is Heavenly Father and Jesus Christ who bless us, through the means of the Savior's infinite Atonement.

## Prayer Not Delegated

One of the most powerful ways to reestablish or strengthen our connection with God is often overlooked because it is so simple. After the Fall of Adam and Eve, Heavenly Father delegated much of the administration of this earthly kingdom to His Son. We refer to the gospel of Jesus Christ, not the gospel of Heavenly Father. We join the Church of Jesus Christ. The Book of Mormon is another Testament of Jesus Christ. We are commanded to come unto Christ. Indeed, "All things which have been given of God from the beginning of the world, unto man, are the typifying of [Christ]" (2 Nephi 11:4).

It is interesting, however, to note that Heavenly Father did not delegate *prayer* to Jesus Christ. Ponder the significance of being not only invited but commanded to talk to the God of the universe—He who directed the creation of worlds without number and who is also our literal Father. He is omniscient and omnipotent, His influence is omnipresent, and still, He wants us to have a direct line to speak with Him. When we pray, we don't teach God anything He doesn't already know—but we learn a great deal about ourselves *and* Him. Prayer is not for God's benefit; it is for ours.

*When we pray, we don't teach God anything He doesn't already know—but we learn a great deal about ourselves* and *Him. Prayer is not for God's benefit; it is for ours.*

Prayer is not something that should be an afterthought or treated superficially. In fact, President Henry B. Eyring taught: "The restored gospel makes plain the simple things we need to do. And it gives us confidence that the help we need will come if we do those things early and persistently, long before the moment of crisis. The first, the middle, and the last thing to do is to pray."[4]

When we pray, our minds can easily "zone out." When this happens, it is natural to pick right up where we left off, as if God doesn't know we let our mind wander. An inspired friend, Cheryl Betenson, taught me a powerful lesson: "How frustrated I would be that I couldn't focus for longer than five minutes before my mind wandered. After some time, I noticed that my mind was wandering to concerns." The things that were drawing her attention *away* from prayer, in many cases, turned out to be the very things about which she needed to pray the most. After this realization, she would use those distracting thoughts as focal points for deeper engagement with Heavenly Father as she sought His counsel more sincerely and specifically. I have applied this principle on many occasions. It has turned "heaven-distancing" situations into heaven-seeking experiences.

Heaven also feels closer when we spend more time talking to Heavenly Father about what we *most* desire in eternity. This principle might be as simple as praying for more than just our physical needs.

We usually ask for a blessing on our food, safety in our travels, and help to do well with the tests we face at home, school, work, or other daily responsibilities. With a little adjustment, we could also thank Him for our "spiritual food" and plead with Him to bless our scripture study to truly nourish and strengthen our souls. We could pray for safety from *spiritual* accident and harm that would take us from the straight and narrow path. While not disregarding the physical requirements of the day, we could also plead for His help to pass our eternally significant tests of faith and consecration.

## Types of Answers

In the second chapter of Ether, the brother of Jared built eight barges that were so "tight like unto a dish" (v. 17) that they had three major problems. He addressed each of these issues in prayer: "O Lord, in them there is no light; whither shall we steer? And also we shall perish, for in them we cannot breathe" (v. 19). The Lord began by giving the brother of Jared step-by-step instructions for how to solve the most pressing problem: how to breathe. Without delay, the brother of Jared acted on those instructions. He didn't insist that the Lord answer the other two questions before he followed the revelation given. Quickly acting on revelation we receive, as incomplete as it may seem, opens the door for additional inspiration.

*Quickly acting on revelation we receive, as incomplete as it may seem, opens the door for additional inspiration.*

After the brother of Jared followed all of the steps outlined by the Lord, he returned and asked again about the other two unresolved issues—steering and light. Rather than telling him how to solve the lighting problem, the Lord activated this prophet's agency. But He didn't expect the brother of Jared to solve the light problem all on his own. He asked, "*What will ye that I should do* that ye may have light in your vessels?" (Ether 2:23; emphasis added). The Lord did not expect the brother of Jared to create light; He expected him to figure out a way the Lord could help provide the needed illumination in the barges. The Lord addressed the third issue by explaining that they would not need to worry about steering because *He* would control their direction using wind and waves.

This story shows a pattern of three different types of answers we can receive when trying to solve problems:

(1) Exact instructions (breathing)
(2) Activation of agency (light)
(3) Assurance to not worry about it (steering)

Answers from the Lord do not always fit neatly into only one of these categories, but these variations can help us make better sense of our own situations. At first thought, we may prefer most of our answers to fall under the "don't worry about it—I'll take care of it" category. However, this type of interaction is best for small children. Adults grow less when God takes care of everything without any effort on their part. The next instinctive preference might be step-by-step instructions for how to solve our problems. If that were always the case, however, life would begin to feel so prescriptive that it could lose much of its interest and significance. Thus, our Heavenly Father often answers us with, "What would you like me to do about that?"

> *Progressively expecting more from a child and empowering him or her to use agency is not a sign of a parent's decreasing concern and involvement but of a parent's love and trust.*

Progressively expecting more from a child and empowering him or her to use agency is not a sign of a parent's decreasing concern and involvement but of a parent's love and trust. The same is true of our connection with our Heavenly Parents. The more spiritually mature we become, the more likely we are to hear, "What would you like me to do about this issue?"

Heaven feels distant for some when they receive silence in response to a sincere, heartfelt petition. From the brother of Jared's perspective, though, this stillness opens the possibility that sometimes our questions are being answered by the Lord trusting us to choose for ourselves what to do. In this light, we are more likely to respond to silence with gratitude rather than frustration or bitterness. At that point, the Lord's trust in us allows us to "study it out in [our] mind" (D&C 9:8) and explore various solutions to our problems.

The brother of Jared could have quickly gathered sixteen random rocks and placed them before the Lord. This would have decreased his confidence in asking Heavenly Father to make the stones shine, however. Instead, he went to significant effort and presented the best solution he could with the resources available to him. At the top of a high mountain, he found materials to melt down and make sixteen smooth, transparent stones. While not as perfect as what the Lord could have made, those sixteen stones represented the brother of Jared's engagement in the process. Because of this, he could approach his Father in Heaven with great confidence and faith when asking Him to touch the stones and make them shine (see Ether 3:1–5).

## Meaning in Silence

We sometimes hear silence as the answer to our prayers not because the Lord trusts us and wants us to use our agency, but perhaps because we lack real intent to act if we were to receive an answer. Elder David A. Bednar taught this principle using Joseph Smith's First Vision as an example: "Joseph's questions focused not just on what he needed to know but also on what was to be *done!* His prayer was not simply, 'Which church is right?' His question was, 'Which church should I join?' Joseph went to the grove to ask in faith, and he was determined to act."[5] Prayers of idle curiosity are more likely to be answered with silence than prayers motivated by a willingness to act in accordance with direction we receive.

*Prayers of idle curiosity are more likely to be answered with silence than prayers motivated by a willingness to act in accordance with direction we receive.*

Another reason for the Lord's silence might, ironically, be a lack of silence *on our part.* It is a natural tendency to fill most of our personal prayer time with talking. The English word *heart* begins with *hear.* In fact, there is an *ear* in the middle of the word *heart.* The most important truths we learn in life will not bounce off our eardrums; they will be sensed by this internal ear, which requires appropriate time for pondering. President Boyd K. Packer taught, "The Holy Ghost speaks with a voice that you *feel* more than you *hear.*"[6] This implies that many of us could benefit from spending more time being still and knowing that He is God (see D&C 101:16) while in the attitude of prayer. Some of our most powerful experiences supplicating Heavenly Father might be when we simply cry at His feet and spiritually reach out to Him with our hearts rather than with words. Paul assured us that "the Spirit itself maketh intercession for us with groanings which cannot be uttered" (Romans 8:26). Gratefully, God doesn't have "office hours"; He has an open-door policy for us to approach His throne of mercy and grace at any time, in any place, for any reason.

We are also more likely to get a response if we ask for more than a laundry list of desires. Personal requests *are* important; indeed, we are commanded to pray over all things in our lives (see Alma 34:18–27). But what difference would it make if we spent more time in prayer seeking to know what Heavenly Father wants from us rather than spending all our time telling Him what He can do for us.

## Windows and Mirrors

As is the case with prayer, Heavenly Father doesn't learn anything new when we study our scriptures, but we do. Referring to the Book of Mormon, President Ezra Taft Benson promised, "There is a power in the book which will begin to flow into your lives the moment you begin a serious study of the book. You will find greater power to resist temptation. You will find the power to avoid deception. You will find the power to stay on the strait and narrow path."[7] We don't have to do this for days, weeks, or years before we feel the power flowing into our lives. President Benson clearly promised we would feel that power the *moment* we begin a serious study.

Just as we might zone out during prayers, we sometimes do the same when reading scriptures. Have you ever read an entire chapter only to realize as you turn the page that you have no idea what any of it said? If we analyze what caused our minds to wander, we might find that we were thinking about something that needs our attention *and* heaven's help. We can reread that same page of scripture while specifically looking for principles to help with the very thing that caused our minds to wander. We may find answers to our struggles in the very words we had glossed over.

One thing that helps decrease our propensity to lose focus while studying the scriptures is to look for relevance in all we read. The scripture pages are like windows that reveal the hand of the Lord in the lives of people and places far removed from us. Windows and scripture pages also have the ability to *reflect*. They can help us see the hand of the Lord mirrored in our own lives. Like multiple windows in a home, each character and story, each sermon and discourse, if given more than a passing glance, offers us a unique and complementary view of God's goodness and power.

Reflections from the scriptures can teach us truths that otherwise remain hidden. At this mirror-like level, scripture *history* actually becomes *ourstory*, and heaven feels closer. We begin to see ourselves and others symbolically personified in the scripture's characters, objects, and events. The more we seek to learn and understand "ourstory," the more complete our outlook becomes and the clearer we see God's hand working in our own life.

## Where Jesus *Walks*

When Jesus was twelve years old, Mary and Joseph lost him in Jerusalem for three days after the Passover. It is hard to imagine what they must have felt when they couldn't find Him. Their deep anxiety and panic were washed away when they finally found Him in the temple. When heaven feels distant today, we can either wait for the Lord to come to us or we can actively seek Him. A good place to begin that search is in the house of the Lord.

> *"It is a holy thing to walk where Jesus walked, but it is a* holier *thing to walk where Jesus* walks.*"*

I learned this lesson in an unforgettable way while attending the sealing of my wife's sister and her husband. They were sealed in the Bountiful Utah Temple, in the same room where my wife and I had been married a few years prior. Their sealer began by sharing that he and his wife had just returned from a trip to the Holy Land. He briefly described how inspirational it had been to visit so many hallowed sites. Then he looked around the beautiful room and reverently said something that went straight to my heart: "It is a holy thing to walk where Jesus walked, but it is a *holier* thing to walk where Jesus *walks*."

## Means and Ends

When seeking the Lord, we must consider the underlying reason *why* we do *what* we do. If we forget why outward activities of Church membership exist, they can easily become *ends* unto themselves. Going to church will not save anyone. Studying scriptures or saying sincere prayers will not exalt us either. Family history research, temple worship, fasting, and magnifying our callings are not salvation. All of these things are how we engage with Christ, who helps us become more like Him and our Father. The commandments were not given just to fill our time or keep us out of trouble; they are opportunities to practice internalizing divine attributes. A group of people in the Book of Mormon understood this: "Now they did not suppose that salvation came by the law of Moses; but the law of Moses did serve to strengthen their faith in Christ; and thus they did retain a hope through faith, unto eternal salvation" (Alma 25:16).

*All of these things are how we engage with Christ, who helps us become more like Him and our Father.*

This perspective gives more depth and purpose to all of the good things we do. We don't go to church out of duty; we go because we urgently need to reconnect with Heavenly Father and the Savior through the sacrament. We go because the fellowship of the Saints allows us an opportunity to learn and remember the truths of the gospel, which give us motivation to work through life's struggles. We go because it gives us a chance to find others who might need our help and encouragement.

When we gain this perspective, we no longer read our scriptures or say our prayers as part of a checklist. We recognize that those things do not feed our souls unless we do them as means to strengthen our faith in Christ and worship God more earnestly. We approach these and all other Church-related activities from the perspective that they are ways for us to build "upon the rock of our Redeemer, who is Christ, the Son of God" (Helaman 5:12). Foundations built on anything but the Savior Himself will eventually fail us, regardless of how good those efforts are.

## Master or Servant

When Church activity or gospel living begins to feel mundane or less meaningful, it is remarkable how fasting refocuses and energizes the process. We may dread the physical discomfort of hunger and thirst associated with fasting, but with some adjustment it can become a true delight. Isaiah asked an important question regarding this law: "Is it such a fast that I have chosen? a day for a man to afflict his soul? . . . wilt thou call this a fast, and an acceptable day to the Lord?" (Isaiah 58:5). He explained that fasting was given to "loose the bands of wickedness, to undo the heavy burdens, and to let the oppressed go free, and that ye break every yoke" (v. 6). He spoke of how fasting opens the channel of communication with the Lord and allows the soul to rise out of darkness (v. 9–11).

We are so accustomed to accommodating demands from our physical body throughout the month that eventually our spirit can become subservient to the flesh. This does not mean our body is evil; it is an amazing gift from the Lord. It just needs to be taught its proper role so it does not overpower our spirit. Once a month, the Lord helps us reset this relationship through the law of the fast. During that time, our body still makes its demands, but our spirit is given the chance to say no. Each request for eating or drinking becomes a reminder of our fast and its purposes. By the end of our fasting experience, our body has become subject to our spirit once again. A proper master/servant relationship is reestablished between the two, and our ability to control other harmful impulses increases.

## Beyond Words

The Lord has given us more than inspired words as ways to feel His love and inspiration. Music, art, and other forms of media have the capacity to open up channels of communication between heaven and the soul that words alone will never know. Many who struggle have found peace and increased revelation by surrounding themselves with inspiring music and media that touch the heart, elevate thoughts, and lift the soul.

We cannot purposely expose our spirits to evil music and media and expect the companionship of the Holy Ghost in our lives. This is not to say we should listen to only church music, visit only LDS websites, or watch only Church-produced movies. But just like planting a garden, we can't plant weeds and expect to one day eat fruit. Wild plants, like degrading media, choke out the good seeds we have planted in our soul.

When I served my mission, I couldn't wait for my time in the MTC to end so I could get out into the field. Once I arrived in Curitiba, Brazil, however, I wished I could go back to the MTC. Everything seemed bleak for me during those first few days. I struggled with the food (my first dinner appointment made me so sick I threw up after we left). I couldn't sleep well at night because of swarming mosquitos and other biting insects. I was surrounded by extreme poverty and filth. I saw young children with skin lesions, wearing rags, missing teeth, and playing in the mud with diseased animals. I saw others being abused by drunk parents. I felt so lost in my new world; the language, the culture, the slums, and the reality of two years staring me in the face created a sense of panic and serious doubt in my ability to effectively endure and serve. I prayed. I pled for strength and peace. I pored over my scriptures, looking for solace and reassurance that I could fulfill this mission. But the desired peace and reassurance was elusive.

Toward the end of that first week, my trainer, Elder Pratt (who was also the zone leader), had to spend a few hours calling all of the missionaries in our zone from the clerk's office in the church. He told me I could spend that time studying the language and my scriptures. I walked into the chapel and instantly felt prompted to go and play some of my favorite hymns on the piano. The next two hours proved to be life changing for me. As I played, the Lord touched my heart in a profound way. My pent-up frustrations and concerns finally started to melt away as I played those hymns and sang along through my tears. The testimony infused in that inspired music melted the discouragement around my heart. This allowed other hope-filled messages to sink deep into my soul, reassurances that I can still feel to this day. The Lord filled me with light, love, and hope. This experience with music enabled me to move forward with faith and confidence that the Lord had not left me alone and that He would always be with me. That was the first of many profound experiences when I have been strengthened through inspired music.

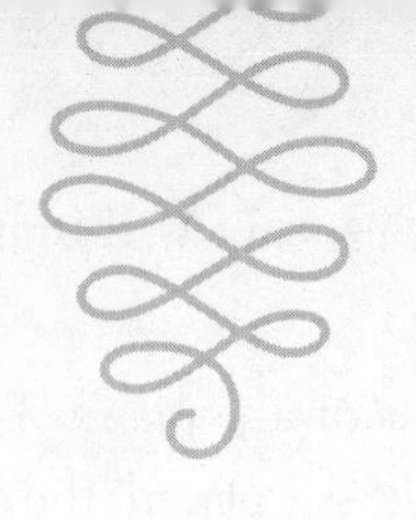

CHAPTER 9

# How Firm a Foundation Is Laid for Our Faith!

*"What more can he say, than to you he hath said,*
*Who unto the Savior for refuge hath fled?"*[1]
*—"How Firm a Foundation"*

As we each wrestle with our unique set of challenges, whether they are caused by Heavenly Parents shaping our character through painful lessons, prolonged wilderness wanderings, less-than-ideal timing, ambiguity, weakness of the flesh, or loved ones who struggle, we can take great comfort in knowing that God is perfectly aware of our situation. His watchful eye is always on us. His care and concern for our eternal progression never wanes. He provided one way for us to be saved: He sent His only perfect Son to become like us, so that we, through Him, could become like Them.

Heavenly Father personally introduced that Son in a grove we now call sacred, to the kneeling and pleading farm boy who would become the great Prophet of the Restoration. That introduction consisted of eight simple words: Joseph, "*This is My Beloved Son. Hear Him!*" (JS—History 1:17). Speaking of that singular event, President Gordon B. Hinckley said, "Do you realize the import of that declaration? Here was God the Eternal Father, the Almighty, bearing testimony in words plainly spoken. No more important or compelling testimony has been given of the risen Lord than this testimony of his own Father."[2]

God Himself has laid a firm foundation for our faith in Him and

His Son. That foundation will strengthen our resolve to never forsake Him, even when fears mount up and strength slackens, in deep waters, through fiery trials, or in old age, when His loving hand continues to shape and polish us.

## In Every Condition

When Benjamin, our first child, was born, I was finishing up college and working two part-time jobs. As the bills began arriving, we had to draw extra funds out of our savings to pay them. I knew this would continue unless we made adjustments to our budget. My wife and I sat down to discuss our funds. She began the discussion by saying, "I think we should put five more dollars into the fast offering fund."

This made absolutely no sense to me. I gently reminded her that we were attempting to cut *back* on our budget. Kiplin responded that she still felt that we should *begin* by adding $5 to our monthly fast offering contribution. I remarked that our current fast offering was already generous for a couple in college and that we could add more money *after* we had decreased expenditures in other categories. She still insisted on starting there. Her unwavering insistence frustrated me. I couldn't figure out why she was struggling to understand basic principles of mathematics. We tabled the issue.

The Saturday before fast Sunday, when I filled out the donation slip and fast offering check, I felt justified in writing it for the amount we had previously budgeted. We had no tithing envelopes on hand, so I temporarily placed the check in our planner. Later that day, Kiplin saw the check and threw her arms around me, thanking me for including the five extra dollars in our fast offering. I was *so* confused. I went back to the planner and looked at the donation slip and noticed that she was right. In my own handwriting, the check was written out for the higher amount. In that moment, almost feeling like my agency had been violated, something unexpected happened inside me. I began to understand basic principles of mathematics—the Lord's way. That experience softened my heart and changed my perspective. We were able to adjust our budget so things worked out. From my dear wife, I learned that the Lord magnifies us and our resources when we appropriately sacrifice a little of the very thing we lack.

*The Lord magnifies us and our resources when we appropriately sacrifice a little of the very thing we lack.*

This same principle applies to more than monetary offerings. When a person is short on time, for instance, he or she could try sacrificing a few moments helping someone else. If another person feels lonely or unloved, he or she could find someone to love and serve a little more and then see what God does with the feelings of love in his or her own life. If members of the Church feel underappreciated or underutilized, they need not wait for a calling to serve. There are always chances for work and opportunities for service, if we are looking for them.

Any offering we make, of any kind, is a small approximation of the Savior's infinite and eternal sacrifice for us. "Though he was rich, yet for your sakes he became poor, that ye through his poverty might be rich" (2 Corinthians 8:9). Now he invites each of us to become a little more like Him through our offerings; we become a little poorer while helping the poor become a little richer.[3]

## "Fear Not, I Am with Thee"

Few scriptures illustrate the principle of God's closeness and mercy better than the book of Hosea in the Old Testament. It contains one of the greatest symbolic love stories ever told. Metaphorically, Hosea represents Jesus, bound through covenant to the house of Israel, represented by Gomer. At a more personal level, however, this is the story of our own covenants with the Lord and our struggles to keep them; in symbolic ways, *we* are Gomer.

The prophet Hosea was commanded to marry "a wife of whoredoms" (Hosea 1:2). Hosea was obedient to the command and married Gomer. They were blessed with three children, all of whom had symbolic names: Jezreel (God sows), Lo-Ruhamah (no mercy), and Lo-Ammi (not my people). Shortly after bearing these children, Gomer became tired of her covenant life with Hosea. She forsook him and went back to her former life as a harlot.

Notice the focus on the self in Gomer's words: "I will go after *my* lovers, that give me *my* bread and *my* water, *my* wool and *my* flax, *mine* oil and *my* drink" (Hosea 2:5; emphasis added). She wanted her former lovers to provide her with bread and water. In a latter-day application, not likely intended by the original author, bread and water take on sacramental significance. She no longer wanted to rely on Hosea for her source of strength and spiritual sustenance. She preferred the instantaneous carnal gratification that her lovers offered. The garments and coverings provided by Hosea were also discarded in favor of her lovers' fashions.

For a short season, Hosea hedged up Gomer's way and made it so she could not find her lovers (see Hosea 2:6–7). To me, the most touching part of the story is what happened next. Hosea would have been justified by the Law of Moses in having her stoned or openly shamed for her betrayal. Instead, he chose to gently persuade her away from her sins, "speak comfortably unto her" and "betroth [her] unto [himself] in righteousness, and in judgment, and in lovingkindness, and in mercies" (v. 14, 19). This part of the story concluded with tender promises from the Lord that are rooted in their children's names, "And I will sow her unto me in the earth; and I will have mercy upon her that had not obtained mercy; and I will say to them which were not my people, Thou art my people; and they shall say, Thou art my God" (v. 23).

Hosea and Gomer's story symbolically encapsulates our covenantal connection with the Lord. He *wants* to be our God, and He *wants* us to be His people. When heaven feels distant due to broken covenants, this story provides hope that it is never too late to reestablish that connection with the Lord. Like Hosea, he will eventually seek after us and invite us back into the safety of His covenant, even if we struggle to return to Him on our own. Elder Jeffrey R. Holland taught:

> However late you think you are, however many chances you think you have missed, however many mistakes you feel you have made or talents you think you don't have, or however far from home and family and God you feel you have traveled, I testify that you have *not* traveled beyond the reach of divine love. It is not possible for you to sink lower than the infinite light of Christ's Atonement shines.[4]

## Through Deep Waters

Another essential connection with heaven is through the Lord's chosen servants. Whenever a dispensation of the gospel has been on the earth, God has communicated with His children through prophets. Unfortunately, the devil also spreads his lies to discredit or explain away God's messages, miracles, and wonders (see 3 Nephi 1:21–22).

A great example to demonstrate this contrast is found near the end of the book of Acts. Paul was being taken by ship to Rome to be judged by Nero, the Caesar. The ship was carrying 276 people, including sailors, prisoners, and soldiers. On the way, they stopped on the south side of the island of Crete at a place called the fair havens. They were late in the year, and the season for sailing in the Mediterranean Sea had passed. They had a decision to make about whether to stay in the fair havens or to go a little farther down the coastline to Phenice for the winter. As they debated the options, Paul spoke up, saying, "Sirs, I perceive that this voyage will be with hurt and much damage, not only of the lading and ship, but also of our lives" (Acts 27:10).

As is often the case with prophets, Paul gave no earthly rationale for his prophecy. At that point, the experts on the ship spoke to the contrary. The centurion believed the captain and owner of the ship rather than trusting Paul. Because the fair havens were "not commodious to winter in, the more part advised to depart thence also" (v. 12). They also reasoned that Phenice was just a short distance to the west, and it had better accommodations for the winter months ahead. The final encouragement to leave came when "the south wind blew softly" (v. 13). Being on the south side of Crete and wanting to sail a short distance to the west, a gentle breeze from the south provided the ideal conditions. Their minds were made up. Against Paul's prophetic counsel, they set sail.

Whenever people disregard the counsel of prophets, negative consequences eventually follow. In this case, the consequences happened almost immediately after the sailors left the fair havens. A tempestuous wind arose, catching the ship in its grip and making it impossible for them to control the sails or rudder. They were at the mercy of the storm. After days of being driven by the tempest, they were forced to lighten the ship by throwing valuable provisions overboard. Paul eventually stood up and calmed the others' fears by telling them that no lives would be lost. He also told them that the ship would be destroyed and they would land on an island. Everyone on the ship believed Paul this time, even though this prophecy should have been more difficult to believe than his first one. All of these prophecies were fulfilled when they landed on Malta. Heaven will feel less distant, even if we are rudderless on a stormy sea, as we heed the words of the Lord's prophets.

The Lord's appointed servants have never claimed infallibility. They are charged with guiding us in the right direction for our day. Our test is not in how many perceived faults we can find in Church leaders and their teachings but rather in how well we follow their divinely inspired counsel and direction. The world will always provide us with ample reasons to discredit or disbelieve what prophets say. But like the soldiers and sailors on Paul's ship, we learn that prophets can see storms and opportunities when they are a great way off.

## Through Fiery Trials

For those who feel alone, hurt, betrayed, forsaken, or ignored, or who don't know if they have any more tears left to cry, there is *always* hope through Jesus Christ. Although heaven feels distant for people in different ways and for different reasons, the reality is that those feelings will not last forever.

The Lord may not take away all our burdens, but He *will* walk our painful roads with us, in life or in death. Mortality's outcomes alone are not a good measure of God's care, concern, and power of deliverance. Peter wrote, "Beloved, think it not strange concerning the fiery trial which is to try you, as though some strange thing happened unto you" (1 Peter 4:12).

Though some are physically spared from literal or symbolic flames, others are not. But *all* who love and follow the Lord are spiritually delivered. The three Hebrews, Shadrach, Meshach, and Abednego, were miraculously saved from Nebuchadnezzar's fiery furnace (see Daniel 3), but Abinadi was delivered to scourging flames in King Noah's court. Abraham's life was saved by an angel on the very same altar where the three daughters of Onitah had been

*God's refining fire may purge for a season, but our pure gold will shine forever.*

sacrificed because of their virtue and unwillingness to worship idols (see Abraham 1:11).

The refining fire might lead to healing for some and death for others. Earthly outcomes are only one possible indicator of the Lord's love and omniscience. God's refining fire may purge for a season, but our pure gold will shine forever.

## "All My People Shall Prove"

John the Baptist's miraculous birth showed that God can shape His children even in the winter of their lives. Elisabeth was barren, and she and Zacharias were both "well stricken in years" (Luke 1:7). Zacharias was performing his priestly duty in the temple by burning incense in front of the veil when an angel appeared and declared, "Fear not, Zacharias: *for thy prayer is heard*; and thy wife Elisabeth shall bear thee a son, and thou shalt call his name John" (v. 13; emphasis added). It seems strange that the angel would say Zacharias' prayer was *heard.* Although it is possible that Zacharias went into the temple that particular day praying for a son, it seems more likely, considering their advanced ages, that the angel was referring to what must have been a commonly repeated prayer throughout many previous decades when Elisabeth and Zacharias were younger. How sealed the heavens must have felt as childless days turned into months, and then years, and finally decades, when likely all hope was finally crushed.

*Even though the Lord knew He would send them one of the most significant children ever to be born, Zacharias and Elisabeth didn't have this assurance throughout their long ordeal.*

Even though the Lord knew He would send them one of the most significant children ever to be born, Zacharias and Elisabeth didn't have this assurance throughout their long ordeal. They had to endure years of childlessness filled with countless unanswered prayers. Elder Jeffrey R. Holland said, "I testify that God lives, that He is our Eternal Father, that He loves each of us with a love divine. I testify that Jesus Christ is His Only Begotten Son in the flesh. . . . They sustain us in our hour of need—and always will, even if we cannot recognize that intervention. Some blessings come soon, some come late, and some don't come until heaven; but for those who embrace the gospel of Jesus Christ, *they come.*"[5]

## Shaping Experiences

I conclude by sharing a few personal experiences that have shaped me and taught me significant lessons about the watchful care of the Lord and the nearness of heaven.

The first took place a few years ago, when I stood holding my father's hand as his spirit slipped into the eternities. He had suffered a major stroke twenty years before that, while I was serving my mission. He spent those last two decades of life wrestling with numerous physical, mental, emotional, and spiritual side effects of his stroke. He often lamented that he couldn't seem to "find the door out of this life." Another stroke finally brought him to that door.

As he lay in a hospital bed, straddling the threshold between this world and the next, I held his hand and placed my other hand on his chest. I could feel his faltering heartbeat and slowing breath, and I introspectively reviewed what I knew about our Heavenly Father's plan of happiness. Heaven was *very* close at that tender moment. As my father's heart finally went still, my own was filled with love for him and for the Savior, who made it possible for our relationship to endure in glory forever. Dad had finally found his passage into the eternities, and by so doing, he helped me find a new connection with heaven that has deepened my relationships with loved ones ever since.

## Santa Socks

Another experience occurred many years ago on Christmas Eve. Two of my young children approached me with a sincere concern. Kinley was five years old at the time and Jarret was three. They told me they had been discussing the fact that Santa always brings everyone presents but never gets any in return. They had decided that this Christmas, they were going to give him a gift in return. I was genuinely touched by their thoughtfulness. Kinley said that they had gone through all of their treasures but couldn't find anything they thought Santa would want. I assured them that their willingness to even consider giving a present would be a significant gift to him.

But they were determined to give him something special. They figured out that *I* had something that Santa might possibly find useful. They asked if I would be willing to let them give a pair of my socks to Santa so he could use them to keep his feet warm during the cold nights at the North Pole. I quickly agreed to this plan. Kinley promptly produced a pair of socks from behind her back that the two had already picked out. They were both a little reticent, however, worrying that my socks might not fit Santa or that he would think this was a silly present. I had a hard time holding back my emotions as I guaranteed them that the socks would be a perfect fit and that Santa would see them as one of the finest presents he had ever received.

"Do you think he will actually wear them?" asked Jarret.

"I can guarantee it!" I responded.

That night, I found a crudely wrapped package with the socks and a card signed by both of them, along with the following message, written in age-typical handwriting: "Dear Santa, Thank you. We love you. Thanks you! P.S. We hope the sock fit. Have fun dilivering present's." Their card will forever be in Santa's collection of treasures.

This experience offered me a profound tutorial as I considered all of the things I had tried to give the Lord. Heaven felt very near as

I realized that each of my gifts to God was embodied in those socks. Kinley and Jarret taught me that the value of a gift to the Lord is not in the object itself; it is our heartfelt thought and childlike desire to give something of value that matters. How God must smile as we ask Him to give us the very things we intend to wrap up and place under His tree, with His name written on the tag, complete with imperfect letters and spelling. Ultimately, everything we offer Him, including the wrapping paper and bows, is already his. The real gift is our expression of love for Him. Elder Neal A. Maxwell said all of our gifts to the Lord "could be stamped justifiably 'Return to Sender,' with a capital S."[6]

## Know the Master

Another experience that brought heaven closer for me occurred during the Easter season of 2008. My wife and I made an effort to teach our children what Jesus experienced on each day throughout that week, beginning with Palm Sunday and ending with Easter morning. Wanting them to walk with Him during His final week two thousand years ago, we would discuss what might have been occurring at various times during each of those days. On Friday evening, we reviewed scriptures recounting the Crucifixion, death, and burial of Jesus. The children built a Lego model of a tomb. We wrapped a small picture of Jesus in a strip of white linen, placed it in the tomb, and sealed it shut. On Saturday, the children kept asking for all the details they could get about Resurrection morning. We went through the related scriptures and reminded them that Jesus would have risen from the dead long before they would wake up on Sunday morning, because it was still dark when Mary went to the tomb and found it empty (see John 20:1). We didn't realize how deeply this exercise had sunk in for our eight-year-old Jacob.

Just after 5:00 a.m. on Sunday morning, our baby, Jarret, began crying in the boys' bedroom. I went in to comfort him and began softly dancing him around the room. With just the slightest hint of light in the room, I glanced up at the top bunk and was startled to see the faint outline of a figure sitting up against the wall. Jacob was wide awake! I asked him why he was sitting up rather than sleeping. He simply responded, "I wanted to be awake when Jesus comes out of the tomb. Would Jesus have been resurrected by now, Dad?"

I was speechless. Through that simple act, my eight-year-old taught me lessons I could never learn from reading books or listening to lectures about the life of Christ. I could almost hear an audible voice in my mind reciting, "For how knoweth a man the master whom he has not served, and who is a stranger unto him, and is far from the thoughts and intents of his heart?" (Mosiah 5:13).

## Conclusion: Never Give Up and Never Forsake!

One final experience that taught me a profound lesson about heaven's nearness involved Jarret when he was almost four years old. I felt frustrated as a parent because he was not yet potty-trained. The previous four children had all mastered this skill at much younger ages, but Jarret was quite comfortable in his diapers. I tried everything I could to motivate him. Finally, the one thing that seemed to get his attention was a promised date with me if he could go for seven days without any accidents. We started and restarted the counter so many times that I began to wonder if I should just scrap the whole idea and let him stay in diapers indefinitely!

Then, he actually succeeded for three days in a row. I finally had hope that he would make it this time. On the fourth day, however, I went upstairs and saw Jarret hunched down on our bathroom floor. I flipped the light on and looked over his shoulder. He was using a few pieces of soggy toilet paper in an attempt to clean up his accident on the floor. I lost my patience and in exasperation exclaimed, "Oh, no!

Did you have *another* accident?" That was not one of my better parenting moments.

Little Jarret instantly broke into giant tears and body-racking sobs. I was still frustrated as I knelt down beside him. I took him into my arms as I assessed the extent of the "damage" to my tile and grout. After a few moments of sobbing, Jarret turned to me with tear-filled eyes and said, "I'm sorry. I was trying to make it to the potty. I'll never get to go on that date with you, will I, Daddy?"

The windows of heaven opened wide in that moment. In an instant, I became Jarret. In my mind's eye, I could see my own desires to do good, accompanied by countless failures. I pictured myself turning to Heavenly Father with the same tears and shaky voice, apologizing for my numerous accidents and wondering if I would ever be able to get that date with *Him.* I was filled with unspeakable love for that small child. I took him into my embrace and cried with him as I reassured him that I would never give up on him or forsake him. I told him that it didn't matter how long it took, we *were* going to get our date together. He felt hope return, and so did his dad.

*In the end, God is not merely seeking to get us into heaven; He is seeking to get heaven into us!*

I helped Jarret clean up the mess. Heavenly Father and Jesus Christ want to take our burdens and help us clean up our messes, too, but we have to be willing to trust Them and let Them help us.

To all who struggle, hold on to the reality that Jesus was not sent to condemn us for our accidents, weakness, and struggles. He was sent to liberate us *from* them and make us celestial. President Thomas S. Monson has counseled, "Be of good cheer. The future is as bright as your faith."[7]

Heaven is not as distant as it seems. In fact, it is getting closer every day! God is not trying to save us from this earth to take us away to heaven. He is bringing heaven here and inviting each of us to be a part of the earth's purifying and sanctifying process. His comforting promise is sure: "And God shall wipe away all tears from their eyes; and there shall be no more death, neither sorrow, nor crying, neither shall there be any more pain: for the former things are passed away" (Revelation 21:4). In the end, God is not merely seeking to get us into heaven; He is seeking to get heaven into *us!*

# Notes


INTRODUCTION: I Don't Understand, But I Will Trust

1. See Jessica Turner, as told to Lynne Crandall, "Power to Persevere," *New Era,* Oct. 2016, 38–41.
2. I first heard this phrase from Savannah Simmons in a youth talk she gave in our ward in 2016.
3. Neal A. Maxwell, "Repent of [Our] Selfishness," *Ensign,* May 1999, 23–25.

CHAPTER 1: Heaven Is Closer Than It Seems

1. M. Russell Ballard, "Stay in the Boat and Hold On!" *Ensign*, Nov. 2014, 89–92.
2. Howard W. Hunter, "Fear Not, Little Flock," *1988–89 Devotional and Fireside Speeches* (Provo, UT: Brigham Young University Press, 1989), 112.
3. Robert D. Hales, "To the Aaronic Priesthood: Preparing for the Decade of Decision," *Ensign,* May 2007, 48–51.
4. Henry B. Eyring, "O Remember, Remember," *Ensign,* Nov. 2007, 66–69.
5. Quentin L. Cook, "Hope Ya Know, We Had a Hard Time," *Ensign,* Nov. 2008, 102–6.
6. Marion D. Hanks, "Changing Channels," *Ensign,* Nov. 1990, 38–41.

CHAPTER 2: Into the Wilderness to Find God

1. C. S. Lewis, *The Screwtape Letters* (San Francisco: Harper, 2001), 37–38.
2. Ibid., 38.
3. David A. Bednar, "Seek Learning by Faith," *Ensign,* Sept. 2007, 61–68.

4. Dallin H. Oaks, "Opposition in All Things," *Ensign*, May 2016, 114–17.
5. Becky shared her story with us in a family home evening.
6. David A. Bednar, "That We Might 'Not . . . Shrink' (D&C 19:18)," CES Devotional for Young Adults, March 3, 2013.
7. See 1 Nephi 12:16 for the angel's description of the river to Nephi.

CHAPTER 3: Cosmic Clocks vs. Earthly Wristwatches

1. Dallin H. Oaks, "Timing," *Ensign*, Oct. 2003, 10–17.
2. Neal A. Maxwell, "Hope through the Atonement of Jesus Christ," *Ensign*, Nov. 1998, 61–63.
3. Neal A. Maxwell, "Remember How Merciful the Lord Hath Been," *Ensign*, May 2004, 44–46.
4. Dieter F. Uchtdorf, "Come, Join with Us," *Ensign*, Nov. 2013, 21–24.
5. Neal A. Maxwell, "Irony: The Crust on the Bread of Adversity," *Ensign*, May 1989, 62–64.

CHAPTER 4: Heavenly Parents, Earthly Children

1. Thomas S. Monson, "Whom the Lord Calls He Qualifies," *Ensign*, July 2013, 10.
2. Dieter F. Uchtdorf, "Your Wonderful Journey Home," *Ensign*, May 2013, 125–29.
3. Jeffrey R. Holland, "None Were with Him," *Ensign*, May 2009, 86–88.
4. Boyd K. Packer, "To Young Women and Men," *Ensign*, May 1989, 53–59.

CHAPTER 5: Moving Forward Despite Ambiguity

1. Virginia H. Pearce shared these insights with me in a personal email based on her address at a Time Out for Women event.
2. Gordon B. Hinckley, "Life's Obligations," *Ensign*, February 1999, 2–5.
3. Dallin H. Oaks, "Witnesses of God," BYU–Idaho Devotional, February 25, 2014.
4. Tom Cherrington and Brent Fillmore introduced me to the idea of horizontal and vertical sources.
5. My friend Mark Weiss taught me this concept.
6. Howard W. Hunter, "The Opening and Closing of Doors," *Ensign*, Nov. 1987, 54–60. President Hunter was using a line from *Don Quixote* by Miguel de Cervantes as the foundation for this statement.
7. Neil L. Andersen, "Faith Is Not by Chance, but by Choice," *Ensign*, Nov. 2015, 65–68.
8. M. Russell Ballard, "To Whom Shall We Go?" *Ensign*, Nov. 2016, 90–92.

9. Gerald N. Lund, "Countering Korihor's Philosophy," *Ensign*, July 1992, 16–21.
10. Joseph Smith, "Letter to the Church and Edward Partridge, 20 March 1839," 12, in *The Joseph Smith Papers*, accessed March 29, 2017, http://www.josephsmithpapers.org/paper-summary/letter-to-the-church-and-edward-partridge-20-march-1839/12.
11. Richard G. Scott, "Using the Supernal Gift of Prayer," *Ensign*, May 2007, 8–11.

CHAPTER 6: Spirit Is Willing; Flesh Is Weak

1. Robert Millet, on *Mormon Identity*, episode 5, http://broadcast.lds.org/ldsradio/pdf/mormon-identity/mormon-identity-ep-05.pdf.
2. William Shakespeare, *As You Like It*, Act 4, scene 3, lines 134–37.
3. From email correspondence.
4. Ibid.
5. Henry B. Eyring, "We Must Raise Our Sights," *Ensign*, Sept. 2004, 14–19.
6. Boyd K. Packer, "Ordinances," *BYU Speeches*, Feb. 3, 1980.
7. See Dallin H. Oaks, "Our Strengths Can Become Our Downfall," *Ensign*, Oct. 1994, 11–19.
8. Neal A. Maxwell, "According to the Desire of [Our] Hearts," *Ensign*, Nov. 1996, 21–23.
9. C. S. Lewis, *Mere Christianity* (New York: Macmillan, 1960), 142.
10. Shared with me in a personal email. Phillip had shared this concept a few times with our ward council.
11. See Bible Dictionary, "Grace."
12. James E. Faust, "A Message to My Granddaughters: Becoming 'Great Women.'" *Ensign*, Sept. 1986, 16–20.
13. C. S. Lewis, *The Chronicles of Narnia: The Voyage of the Dawn Treader* (London: HarperCollins Children's Books, 2014), 115.
14. Ibid., 115–16.

CHAPTER 7: When Loved Ones Struggle

1. Vaughn J. Featherstone, "A Man After God's Own Heart" *BYU Speeches*, Sept. 12, 1995.
2. Joseph Smith, "Poem to William W. Phelps, February 1843," 82–83, in *The Joseph Smith Papers*, accessed March 29, 2017, http://www.josephsmithpapers.org/paper-summary/poem-to-william-w-phelps-february-1843/1.

3. Gordon B. Hinckley, "The Dawning of a Brighter Day," *Ensign*, May 2004, 81–84.
4. Joseph Smith, "Journal, December 1842–June 1844; Book 1, 21 December 1842–10 March 1843," 157, in *The Joseph Smith Papers*, accessed March 29, 2017, http://www.josephsmithpapers.org/paper-summary/journal-december-1842-june-1844-book-1-21-december-1842-10-march-1843/165.
5. Ibid., 159.
6. Jeffrey R. Holland, "Behold Thy Mother," *Ensign*, Nov. 2015, 47–50.
7. N.T. Wright, a New Testament scholar, has written and spoken much on this subject. For instance, he said, "At no point do the resurrection narratives in the four Gospels say, 'Jesus has been raised, therefore we are all going to heaven.' It says that Christ is coming here, to join together the heavens and the Earth in an act of new creation" (accessed on April 15, 2017, at http://content.time.com/time/world/article/0,8599,1710844,00.html).
8. See D. Todd Christofferson, "As Many as I Love, I Rebuke and Chasten," *Ensign*, May 2011, 97–100.
9. Jeffrey R. Holland, "Look to God and Live," *Ensign*, Nov. 1993, 13–15.

CHAPTER 8: "Draw Near unto Me and I Will Draw Near unto You"

1. Ezra Taft Benson, "Jesus Christ—Gifts and Expectations," in *Speeches of the Year, 1974* (Provo, UT: Brigham Young University Press, 1975), 313.
2. Joseph Smith, in *The Joseph Smith Papers*, accessed March 29, 2017, http://www.josephsmithpapers.org/paper-summary/history-1838-1856-volume-e-1-1-july-1843-30-april-1844/346.
3. Eliza R. Snow, "O My Father," *Hymns* (1985), no. 292.
4. Henry B. Eyring, "In the Strength of the Lord," *Ensign*, May 2004, 16–19.
5. David A. Bednar, "Ask in Faith," *Ensign*, May 2008, 94–97.
6. Boyd K. Packer, "Personal Revelation: The Gift, the Test, and the Promise," *Ensign*, Nov. 1994, 59–62.
7. Ezra Taft Benson, "The Book of Mormon—Keystone of Our Religion," *Ensign*, Nov. 1986, 4–7.

CHAPTER 9: How Firm a Foundation Is Laid for Our Faith!

1. "How Firm a Foundation," *Hymns* (1985), 85.
2. Gordon B. Hinckley, in *Special Witnesses of Christ* (DVD, 2003).
3. My friend and colleague Wayne Dymock shared this insight with me.

4. Jeffrey R. Holland, "The Laborers in the Vineyard," *Ensign*, May 2012, 31–33.
5. Jeffrey R. Holland, "An High Priest of Good Things to Come," *Ensign*, Nov. 1999, 36–38.
6. Neal A. Maxwell, "Consecrate Thy Performance," *Ensign*, May 2002, 36–38.
7. Thomas S. Monson, "Be of Good Cheer," *Ensign*, May 2009, 89–92.

# Index

Index

# About the Author

BYU Photo

TYLER J. GRIFFIN is an associate teaching professor in Brigham Young University's Department of Ancient Scripture. He joined the BYU faculty in 2010 and loves the opportunity this job gives him to interact with over 1,000 students each semester and to present at Education Week every August. Before coming to BYU, he earned a bachelor's degree in electrical/computer engineering and master's and doctorate degrees in instructional technology. He taught in the seminaries and institutes for fifteen years, where he also trained potential seminary teachers and developed an online home study seminary program. Tyler cofounded and codirects the BYU VirtualScriptures.org Group, which produces immersive digital learning tools for enhancing scripture study. He and his wife, Kiplin, are the parents of ten children.